MW00975199

the first term

by

w. shin

The First Term

Copyright © 2011 by W. Shin

For information about reprints or other enquiries, please contact:
wshin484@gmail.com

All scripture quotations, unless otherwise indicated, are taken from the Holy Bible, New
International Version®, NIV®. Copyright ©1973, 1978, 1984, 2011 by Biblica, Inc.™
Used by permission of Zondervan. All rights reserved worldwide. www.zondervan.com

Cover and interior book design by Tallgrass Media.

All rights reserved.
No part of this book may be reproduced in any form or by any electronic or mechanical
means including information storage and retrieval systems, without permission in writing
from the author. The only exception is for short excerpts quoted in a book review.

First Printing: June 2011

ISBN 978-1-4611-4663-6

ACKNOWLEDGEMENTS

I am thankful to God for saving me,
calling me, using me for China.

I am thankful for our family, brothers and sisters.
Your prayer and love are a blessing to us.

I am thankful for our supporting churches for their
precious support and prayer for us and China.

I am thankful to our faithful friends and mentors.
Your encouragement has given us strength,
and your mentoring has given us wisdom.

I am thankful for George and Annette Murray,
and for our professors at Columbia International University.
Through your service and dedication we have learned
how to follow the Lord. We love and respect you.

I am thankful to our mission agency for
serving, praying, and caring for us.

I thank KS and JG for helping me
with the wonderful editing and cover design for the book.

I am thankful for Holly Jo, my niece.
She helped me greatly in urgent translation work.

I pray this book will help and challenge to
readers for their effective ministry.

Praise the Lord!

INTRODUCTION

Modern missions depends much on strategies and methods of the past. However, the world is changing rapidly, and people's worldviews and ideas are changing just as rapidly. Culture has become more accessible through the development of the Internet. Information available online has reduced the information gap between the mission field and the home country. How are we going to effectively do missions in this new era? What are the adequate strategies for modern missions? What preparatory works are necessary to implement these strategies? How are we going to sensitively follow the strategy of modern missions led by the Holy Spirit? What are new ways to evangelize and nurture? This book will provide practical help, insight and inspiration to answer such questions.

Many people think of the first term as a period during which they simply learn a new language, befriend some locals, and travel around the host country. However, this is a misconception. We can also evangelize, nurture as much as we want and plant churches during the first term. Such activities will assist us in learning the language and adapting to the host culture. This book will be a realistic testimony to these convictions and will act as a small guidebook.

There are five reasons why I wrote this book:

1. To give practical help to those going to the mission field, during the first term: what to do, how to live, and how to spend and control time for learning language, beginning ministry, and caring for the family.

2. To help those going to the mission field know how to prepare strategically, culturally, spiritually, materially, financially, and relationally in order to adjust well to the new culture.

3. To provide various examples on how to be able to effectively share the unchanging content of the gospel in cross-cultural situations.

4. To highlight and communicate the importance of creative ministry development in the mission field.

5. To share our experiences during our first term and on preparing for furlough.

22 STRATEGIES A FIRST-TERM MISSIONARY MUST KNOW

In 2005, when we were about to leave for China, our mission agency was just starting its ministry there. Prior to starting my first term, I asked senior field missionaries multiple times about ways to prepare for a successful first term. They, however, gave me no satisfactory answers; they just said simplistic things like "Just come," "You will learn from experience," and "We will tell you during orientation."

With a burdened heart, I took my family to the mission field. The fellowship and exchange of information among missionaries was very much restricted at the time, and is still a problem today. I was unable to meet any missionaries who were familiar with the mission strategies, the ministry philosophy and principles I wanted to implement. The orientation my peers and I received was as general as the information we could easily obtain online. Some information frightened and even discouraged us. Most of the sources were outdated and not properly cited.

We prayed and asked for the guidance and wisdom of the Holy Spirit. Based on what I had learned at Columbia International University (CIU), I set up systematic goals I hoped would help me achieve the vision I had received from God. I also set strategies that were appropriate to the culture and circumstances of the Chinese people living in the 21st century. Moreover, as I was learning the Chinese language, I came up with an approach to cross-cultural interaction, methods of evangelization, and nurturing materials that could help the Chinese people understand the Gospel. With audacity and faith, my wife and I shared the Gospel to those who were brought to us by the Holy Spirit. Yet we were careful about our actions as well. The people we have led to God were nurtured and became the leaders of small groups, and most of them became church leaders who then went on to establish home-based churches.

During the first term, my wife and I, as well as fellow workers we had nurtured together, were able to share the Gospel to about 600 Chinese people who accepted Jesus Christ as their Savior. More than 90% of them had never heard of the Gospel in their entire life. In this section, I have recorded a simplified version of the principles I used while working together with my co-workers during my first term in China. I believe that these 22 principles will be of practical help to those who are going into the mission field for their first time, as well as to the sending churches and mission organizations.

Following are the 22 strategies that I believe a first-term missionary must know:

1. **Actively use the advantages that come from having a geographically neighboring culture.** Japan, China, Korea and Mongolia belong to a single geographical culture. The United States, Canada, Mexico and countries in Central America also belong to a single geographical culture. African countries with a high percentage of Christians and other countries nearby belong to another geographical culture. Often, countries in one geographical culture either share a border or are in close geographical proximity to each other. Historically, they might have had diverse cultural exchanges or tribal mixture; or use the same language or one in conjunction with another. Linguistically speaking, Korea and Japan each have their own language but use Chinese characters in combination. In such countries with a geographical culture, people can easily adapt to the new surroundings. Though it differs depending on individual abilities, people can also master a foreign language within a year to the degree that they can evangelize, nurture, and establish a church.

   We should not underestimate missions in geographically close countries. The Holy Spirit's strategy is to use the growth of churches in geographically close countries to spread the gospel to neighboring countries. For example, the primary mission burdens of Korean churches are Korea's neighboring countries: Japan, China, Mongolia, southeastern Russia and North Korea. All of them bear relationships to the borders by land or sea, or share cultural and ancestral similarities.

2. **Accept the fact that we cannot completely resemble the locals.** Many missionaries have tried to become like the locals. Inability to accomplish this can lead to frustration and despair, and even cause some to leave the mission field. However, we need to be more humble and wise. There are things we cannot do despite our prayers and endeavors. A Caucasian cannot become an Asian or an African. The most important things are to understand the culture of the native

people, to respect their way of life, to love them as our spiritual brothers and sisters created in God's image and to resemble each other in heart. It is essential not just to pursue a physical lifestyle resemblance, but to resemble the locals at heart.

3. **Work with your family as a team.** Local people tend to open up easily and be more generous toward children. Adult foreigners, according to the norms and cultures of each country, may be considered dangerous figures or subjects of surveillance. However, even such people who are exclusive of adult foreigners are typically in favor of their children learning a new language and befriending children of other cultures.

4. **Linguistic incompetence is an inadequate reason for non-evangelization.** It is wrong to ascribe failure in evangelization to language problems, because fluency in a foreign language is not the only factor that leads to successful evangelism. A good way to justify that statement is to look back on how much you evangelized in your own country using your mother tongue. When you firmly believe that someone has been sent to you by the Holy Spirit, you must build a relationship with the person and share the gospel. In fact, the number of people being witnessed to while learning a foreign language may be greater than that after one has mastered the language. Once people have learned the language, they tend to naturally focus on nurturing and teaching.

5. **Open your home.** A mission field is a site of spiritual warfare. Soccer games played at home have a higher likelihood of winning. However, in away games, even a powerful soccer team tends to be easily defeated by a weak team that is not performing at its usual level of ability. When I open my home to others, they begin to open their hearts up. Although my mission field was a country where danger was apparent when opening one's home, in fact, this open home method was the greatest help to mission work and planting churches. Of course, prayer and wisdom are necessary. However, if you start by building friendships, building the church is not at all difficult.

6. **Do not be greedy about mission work—do what you can.** On the mission field, it is wise to perform mission works according to your

talents and the vision given by God rather than to compare yourself with other missionaries. As a result, respect among the missionaries blossoms and team ministry becomes more effective.

7. **When planting a church in a mission field, start as an indigenous church.** Indigenization is more difficult to do later than earlier. The later it takes place, the more difficult the handing over of a church to a local leader becomes due to a lingering affection or distrust. In reality, there are many churches that shut down after a local leader has taken over the reigns. It is because local leaders have not yet been trained in pastoral ministry (they have only studied theology). In order to prevent such an outcome, work with the locals from the beginning.

8. **Develop new nurturing materials appropriate for the nationals, and design a new form of mission.** Do not excessively rely on books or materials brought from your home country. Those materials are not wrong, but they are not necessarily suitable because they are not originally made for a culture other than your own. Develop new materials that the target people can understand well and apply to their real life situation.

In addition, our missions strategy needs to keep up with the increasing diversification and specialization of jobs. In the early missions stage, we began with the coastal approach to missions. This was followed by the inland missions strategy. What we now need is a holistic approach to missions. I believe that the next stage of missions ought to be called the "effective and efficient" stage. To effectively do missions under restricted conditions we need to form "specialized" churches, such as those for CEOs, white-collar workers, entertainers, students, artists, academics, and so on.

I believe that such "specialized" churches are justified due to the limited abilities and restricted working conditions of missionaries. Even though our scope may be demographically narrow, our corresponding influence need not be. As we train CEOs in biblical matters, they are able to influence their employees, and also can be BAM (Business as Mission) missionaries. Professors would be able to steer their students in the right direction. Entertainers can be good role models for their fans. We can train people to reach out within their natural social circle. But first, they need to be discipled so that they can reproduce Christlike followers. A new form of missions means doing it effectively and efficiently.

9. **Learn a foreign language from real life.** Learn a language at school or in the marketplace, with a home tutor and with friends, through programs on television (such as soap operas and movies) as well as while evangelizing, serving in the church and making friends.

10. **Exercise regularly and build up your physical strength.** Maintaining physical strength is essential. When it comes to eating, wisdom and cleanliness are necessary. Often local foods are fine for the nationals but may cause foreigners to develop a disease.

11. **Complete a ministry cycle within the first term.** The cycle begins with sharing the gospel. Converts are then nurtured and once you have a few of them, you can form a small group. As your small groups grow, the next goal is to plant a church. As the church grows and matures, the final goal is to reproduce.

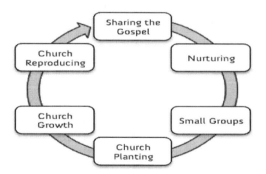

12. **Pray in faith.** Powerful spiritual warfare occurs in the mission field. The existence of the evil spirits is no longer a topic of imagination or debate but of reality. But remember that Satan is afraid of a missionary. The Holy Spirit's work of regenerating life occurs in every passing step of a missionary. No single word of a missionary falls onto the ground and goes rotten. Everything is connected to the history of the gospel.

13. **Individualized disciple training is more effective.** Because people are all different, and each person has a different family culture and

worldview, the individualized format of disciple training rather than a fixed, rigid format has the power to change and grow individuals.

14. **Put all of your effort into the salvation and change of a man.** If you nurture a new convert effectively, you gain a local fellow worker right away. If a man is saved and changed, one nation can change, too. Therefore, one life has more value than the whole universe.

15. **Sharing the gospel cannot be illegal.** About 130 years ago, sharing the gospel in Korea was illegal. If no one had attempted to share the gospel because it was against the law, Korea could not have become a mission powerhouse. (The Korean church is the second largest in sending missionaries after the United States; it has sent over 20,000 missionaries all over the world, *Korean Mission Magazine*.) Of course, one should respect and follow the laws of the host country. However, the gospel is a higher law commanded by God and must be followed. Nonetheless, humility and wisdom are necessary in sharing the gospel.

16. **Plant a church that will not disappear even after a century.** In order to do this, a missionary must lay the foundation of faith on the right track. This means that true disciples and true dedicators for the gospel must be produced. A planted church should not become a momentary church that will disappear once a missionary leaves. Rather, it should become a church where the gospel's genuine essence and power is alive and continued through the generations of dedicators. Every missionary must strategize his mission work using God's words in Romans 15:20 as a basis: *"and thus I make it my ambition to preach the gospel, not where Christ has already been named, lest I build on someone else's foundation."*

17. **Perform a service-based ministry with parents' leadership.** Do not get angry and disappointed at the slow change taking place in the congregation of the mission field. Acknowledge that even a small change is a remarkable growth, taking into account that sinful cultures and idol worship have had a strong grip on people's hearts. Do not expect the same level of Christian culture as in your home country. It will take more than a century for a Christian culture to take root. Encourage and serve those who are amazed at the impressive changes done by God who works in their culture.

18. **Start practicing 'Jesus-likeness' yourself.** The locals meet Jesus Christ and understand the gospel through a missionary. So a missionary must live an exemplary life. However, your life should not emphasize legalism but always be evangelical, focusing on the love of Christ.

19. **Focus on God's glory and worship.** Establishing a church in a mission field is not a matter of choice; it is a requirement. Worship must be full of God's presence and glory. The ultimate goal of missions is for the locals to accept Jesus Christ as their Savior and worship God.

20. **Do not give the local people money but provide them with an opportunity to work.** If a missionary always helps those in need of money, they will consequently rely on the missionary, and not on God. Also, they may develop a habit of resolving every problem with money, not with faith. According to a Chinese proverb, "Don't give a fish, but rather teach him a way to fish". It means "Give a man a fish; you have fed him for one day. Teach a man to fish; and you have fed him for a lifetime." I think this adage is a fundamental lesson for today's missionaries. With patience and dependence on God, give the locals an opportunity to work autonomously and teach them technology so that they can work and earn money.

21. **Build a local church building using local finances.** A church is built with a congregation's prayers, offerings, and labors. As long as it is not in the midst of a primeval jungle where a currency does not exist, build the local church building using the capital of the country in the mission field. By doing so, the indigenization of the church is facilitated, and the independence of the local church and its reproduction also becomes versatile. The same principle holds true when building schools, hospitals, orphanages and welfare facilities for the host country: the less external capital used, the better it is.

22. **Keep the church's budget transparent.** Most people in modern times love money and regard it as important. To nonbelievers money is a subject of veneration. Missionaries must always maintain accuracy and transparency when using the church's finances.

MY MINISTRY PLAN FOR CHINA MISSIONS

1. My Vision from God

A dream comes from oneself. However, a vision comes from God. Sometimes we get these two things confused. We should not pray for our dreams to come true but walk in obedience toward God's vision for us. Then God will achieve His vision for our lives in His time using His ways through our submission. **My vision is to serve the Chinese people with the gospel.**

2. Goals to achieve the vision

1. To equip members to be able to share the Gospel (evangelism training).
2. To plant one church per year
3. To nurture 12 fellow workers during the first term (2 Timothy 2:2)
4. To build a Christian CEO network and training center
5. To teach principles for raising a healthy Christian family
6. To form Intercessory prayer Team of each church
7. To establish CMTC (China Mission Training Center) for sending Chinese missionaries to other countries

3. Values that help to achieve the goals

1. A biblical standard of life
2. Sharing the gospel
3. Discipling and training (church members and CEOs)
4. Use of spiritual gifts
5. Focus on families (Christian education)
6. Prayer and faith
7. Cross cultural training through mission trip of members

4. Target City: Beijing (Capital)

5. Target Groups: The Han Chinese (1.2 billion) and the Japanese community.

6. **Target social strata**: Elites and middle class.

7. **My gifts: Evangelism, serving people, teaching, counseling, preaching, leadership, creativity.**
When we went to the mission field in obedience to God, the Holy Spirit not only gave us many new gifts, but also enhanced the gifts we already had. We were better able to use the gifts with which we were already familiar.

8. **Ministry Philosophy**

   • Romans 15:20, that I would not be building on someone else's foundation.
   • Laying a foundation for a church that would be stable even after a century.
   • Nurturing those who are devoted to God.
   • Faith missions.
   • Team ministry, especially with the local fellow workers believers.

9. **Leadership Pursuits**

   • Leadership of love: to minister with hearts of parents
   • Leadership of serving: to serve others with humility and sincerity
   • Leadership of example: Christlikeness

10. **God's words to me**
"For whoever wants to save his life will lose it, but whoever loses his life for me and for the gospel will save it." – Mark 8:35

IMPORTANCE OF CHINA MISSIONS

1. **China has 13 million atheists.**
   Atheists in China outnumber those in the rest of the world combined. However, we do not have enough missionaries in China, where more than half of the world's missionaries ought to be.

2. **China borders fourteen countries.**
   China's population plus those of her neighboring countries make up more than 3.1 billion people (China—1.4 billion; India—1.1 billion; Russia and Bangladesh—0.3 billion; ten other countries—0.3 billion). This is approximately half of the world's population. This means that as the gospel begins to spread in China, there are 3.1 billion people to be reached in China itself as well as her neighboring countries. (For example, as Korea was evangelizing, it influenced its neighboring countries: China, Japan, Mongolia and eastern Russia. In fact, there are many Korean missionaries working for the Gospel in these countries today.) Therefore, the mission work in China is missiologically very important for Asian missions.

3. **Mission work in China reaches three of the world's major religions.** Two of the world's major religions—Buddhism and Islam—co-exist in China while Hinduism is a major religion in some of China's neighbors. Therefore, one can simultaneously reach these three major religions through missions in China.

4. **The dragon is worshiped in China.**
   "The great dragon was hurled down—that ancient serpent called the devil, or Satan, who leads the whole world astray" (Revelation 12:9). "Then the dragon was enraged at the woman and went off to make war against the rest of her offspring—those who obey God's commandments and hold to the testimony of Jesus" (Revelation 12:17). In the Bible, the dragon refers to Satan (Rev. 12:9). China is an exemplary country that has traditionally worshiped the dragon. It is a place where the spiritual battle is intense and many missionaries who are well prepared and trained are needed.

SEVEN QUESTIONS FOR CHINA MISSION

1. **Home Church:** How can we help to grow the home church into a healthy church that harmonizes a healthy faith, theology and life?

2. **Creative Ministry:** How can we create and develop new ministries while securing and maintaining our current businesses at the same time in the midst of a quickly changing world?

3. **Governmental Ministry:** How are we going to work with the government to help it become more open to Christianity?

4. **Patriot Church Ministry:** How can we help the 15 million members of the Three-Self Church (三自 Three-self: 自传-self-teaching and -propagating，自养-self-supporting，自治-self-governing) take on the responsibilities of the church?

5. **Ministry of Alienated Group:** How are we going to serve those who are neglected?

6. **Minority Ministry:** How can we effectively spread the gospel to 55 different ethnic groups of diverse religions?

7. **World Mission Participation:** How can we help Chinese churches with a total of 90 million saints get involved in world missions?

The following is an account of my first term. You can find out how the strategies, principles, and questions I have raised above are applied to my actual ministries according to the leading of the Holy Spirit in China as you read on.

THE BEGINNING OF MY FIRST TERM

At the start of anything new, there is always anticipation, worry, recklessness, conviction, anxiety and faith. We, too, were there in the beginning. In Beijing, where my family had settled, there was a sense of both the familiar and unfamiliar. We desired to see the light of the hope Jesus had prepared for us and to see ways in which our numerous, long-lifted prayers for China would be confirmed. We tried to pursue God's righteousness in every situation. We strove to apply things we had learned from previous training and to practice them while absolutely relying on God.

We sent out quarterly letters and reports to churches that sponsored us. This section includes letters we sent to sponsoring churches in the first term. Our experiences during the first term, strategies we invented and principles of ministry are explained throughout this section. Jesus Christ guided and used us to build His church one by one just like the Holy Spirit used the evangelists in the book of Acts. The story begins in August 2005 when we arrived in Beijing, China.

OUR INTRODUCTION TO CHINA

When we arrived in Beijing for the first time, my first impression was, "This doesn't look like a mission field." Apart from the Chinese words written on the buildings, Beijing just seemed like any ordinary modern city. The apartments were better built than I had expected and the living environment seemed to be fairly good. I felt sorry when I thought of those who had promised to pray for us thinking that we would face real hardship living in Beijing. Although our first impressions of Beijing were positive, our thoughts changed within a few months.

In my case, even though we were eating Korean food in the mission field, I was suffering from a stomach disorder and diarrhea. Because of this, I couldn't sleep and lost weight.

My wife took 30 different allergy tests at a hospital in Korea and found out that she had a sensitivity to dust that produced severe symptoms. She had had this allergy since we lived in the United States. We found out that Beijing has a lot of dust because of the lack of rain, and because of this, her allergy became worse. Red spots appeared all over her body, and her eyes were so sore that she couldn't open them. Watching my wife suffer was unbearable, and all I could do was pray.

As I was praying and reading the Bible, I happened to come across Matthew 18:19, which says, "Again, I tell you that if two of you on earth agree about anything you ask for, it will be done for you by my Father in heaven." I realized that it is very difficult for two people to agree upon something and pray for something with a sincere heart and desire. So my wife and I started to pray for her health every single day from then on. Astonishingly, God answered our prayers, and my wife's symptoms seemed to get better. Nevertheless, we continued to pray because she had to face the dust whenever she left the house to go outside.

The traffic in China was very dangerous. They seemed to give priority to people driving motorcycles and cars, rather than to pedestrians. People had to run to safety because of all the rough driving. Many Chinese people drove as if they were riding horses, and there was no order in the streets. They ignored the traffic lights and pedestrian crossings; they just drove right through them. As a result, it was very dangerous to walk my kids through all the chaos, but it was necessary because they didn't know Chinese and couldn't read the signs to find their way home. Going out with them left us exhausted because of the stress of trying to keep them safe. It was also nerve-wracking to consider how often children get kidnapped.

For security reasons, there were people monitoring the elevators and all the households, especially the homes of foreigners. It was difficult to let people into the house. Even though they worked as nannies or housekeepers, there was a chance that they might steal things, thinking that foreigners were wealthy and have valuable possessions. One of the most frightening things was the fact that all the Internet services, telephone lines, and letters we received every day were all tapped and monitored. It was as if we were living in a large prison, isolated from the rest of the world.

Learning the Chinese language was a rapid process. We began with me studying at a foreign language institute and my wife studying at an academy and through the help of a tutor. Taking care of the kids and studying at the same time was not an easy task. I was concerned for my wife's health, because she would often get less than four hours of sleep at night.

About eight months into our stay in Beijing, I started attending the morning session of the language school and my wife, the afternoon classes. In the morning, my wife would take the kids to kindergarten. Later that afternoon, I would take them home. At night, a tutor would come over to our house to teach us Chinese, and then we would have about 40 minutes of family worship. The kids would go to sleep after that and I would go back to my study to do homework and prepare for the next lesson the following morning. Our ability to learn the Chinese language progressed and advanced each day. Our kids also began to improve on their Chinese, while still learning more of the Korean language.

After the morning lectures were over, we would sit through another three-hour lecture on studying the language into which the Bible has been translated. In China, the words used in the Bible are very different from the everyday Chinese language. We needed to study the language in depth in order to teach the gospel to others.

Business transactions in China were not only strange, but also ridiculous. A merchant would look at a customer and, if it was a local person, they would give them the local cheap price. But if it was a Korean person, they would give a price four or five times more expensive than the local price. So even if you were able to haggle them down to half the price they gave, it was still at least twice as expensive as the price for a local person.

I bought a bag for my wife when she first started language school. It was priced at 300 Wien, but I bargained it down to 100 Wien. When my wife came home from language school, the first thing she told me was, "There is someone in my class who has the exactly same bag, so I asked her how much she got it for. She told me that she got it for 35 Wien."

The goal was to make a bargain with the store owner down to 1/3 of the quoted price, because he and I both knew that the price he put up wasn't its true price in the first place. If the store owner wasn't willing to bargain, I just had to walk away from the store. Then the store owner would ask me to stay and lower his price. In order to buy a product at the local price, this routine had to be repeated over and over. Every time I wanted to buy something, I felt that I would be ripped off no matter what. It was very tiring and irritating. I prayed that one day, China would become a place where everyone would give an honest price when they were selling things.

CHILDREN ON THE MISSION FIELD

My children had a difficult time adjusting to their new lives in China. One by one, they seemed to catch cold and be very stressed out with adjusting to the new environment. Within a month, they developed disobedient attitudes, and became very rude and violent. Sometimes I felt as though we were living with someone else's kids. Even though they were attending kindergarten and elementary schools, they seemed to get hurt occasionally and learned bad habits from the other kids at school. I realized then that our children were not necessarily living in a safe environment.

My eldest child, Segi, who was six years old at the time, kept telling me that he wanted to go and live in the States. I asked him why, and his answer was, "In the U.S., there are loads of cars so that you can get around anywhere you want, but over here there aren't many cars around. I have to be at home, and it is boring watching TV all day." (He found watching TV boring because it was in Chinese which he found difficult to understand.) I felt sorry for him. We wouldn't let the kids go outside because of the danger and risk of them being kidnapped. So, the children had a very simple lifestyle, coming straight home from school every day.

Then one day, something exciting happened to Segi, an opportunity that would make him love living in China. The kindergarten that he was attending was going to have a cooking competition for dads. The first prize was a bicycle, and my son wanted it really badly. Since the day he heard about the competition, he couldn't stop thinking about the bicycle. He made me fill out and send in the application form for the competition. Once I sent the application form, I couldn't stop thinking about the competition, either. I had to think of or make up a dish that I could cook really well. On the other hand, day by day, my son's desire to have the bicycle grew and grew to the point that he kept shouting to God, "Please give me the bicycle, please give me the bicycle!"

On the day of the competition, I wasn't quite as excited as my son. I walked into Segi's classroom and in front of me I saw 26 grown men sitting in tiny chairs awaiting instructions for the competition. I thought, "Man, this is going to be tough…" and looked at my son. He wasn't looking at me; his eyes were glued to the bicycle.

The dish I was going to cook was a seafood dish using shrimp and prawns. I had mastered this dish at a part-time job while studying abroad. As I prepared the dish, I explained how to carefully take out the insides of the shrimp using nothing but toothpicks. I told the children that the end of the tail should be in such a shape that it appeared to be a high-class dish, how to slice the back of the shrimp in order for it to cook well inside and out, and the fact that the taste differs between a shrimp dish with the heads removed and a dish with the heads still on. Of course, all of this was merely my way of impressing the judges. After the judges had tasted the dishes, the kids started shouting "Bicycle! Bicycle!" I told my son, "All the children have prayed to God that they could have the bicycle. Only God knows whom He is going to give the bicycle to. So, even if the bicycle doesn't end up in your hands, you shouldn't feel bad because everything is in God's hands." I don't think my son thought through what I had just told him, because he kept screaming "No! That bicycle should be given to me! That is mine!" After he calmed down a little bit, he spoke in a shaky voice, "Heavenly Father, please give that bicycle to me." I dreaded the unbearable and awkward situation that I was sure to come.

Soon, all the rewards and prizes were handed out; then, finally, the grand prize was about to be given. At that moment, my son held his breath and time seemed to have stopped. Then one of the judges said, "The grand prize will be given to… Segi's dad!" As soon as my son heard those words, he ran across the room and received the bicycle with pride. Even he couldn't believe that he had won it. I had a huge sigh of relief after he received the prize. I thought for a long time that I wouldn't forget the face of my son, proud and happy.

On the way home, my son felt as if he was about to fly through the skies over Beijing. He was screaming with joy while riding his brand new bicycle. I asked my son, "China isn't that bad, is it?" and my son answered, "Of course not, Dad, I love it. I am going to live in China for long, long time!"

My other son Dan felt so envious of his brother that he asked one of the judges to give him a bicycle as well. The judges felt bad and said they couldn't do that. I think the judges regretted saying that after seeing Dan crying his eyes out and screaming, "You gave my brother one, why not me?" So I took Dan to a bicycle shop and bought him a brand new bicycle. We found one that was both well-built and inexpensive – roughly 33 U.S. dollars. On the way home, I remembered the time my father bought me a bicycle from Seoul and brought it all the way home to Gwang-ju by taking a long trip on the train.

Watching my kids grow day by day, riding their bicycles at a Beijing park, I felt thankful for all the things God gave to our family.

Our two sons would come up to me every now and then and say, "Let's go to the United States" or "Let's go to Korea." Our kids seemed to miss the time they were in the States and in Korea, but thankfully, they did not go beyond asking me every now and then.

THE BEGINNING OF OUR MINISTRY

Our mission agency advised us to focus on studying and learning the language and culture during our first two years in the mission field. So for the first two years, we did not set up any specific plans. However, we felt that if the Holy Spirit started to lead us in a certain direction, we would obey and head toward that path.

The first week, we attended an international church that had approximately 3,000 members representing 60 different countries. That morning they announced that a Japanese church was about to be planted in Beijing. This was very exciting news for me, because our mission target was first for the Han, a Chinese people group, and then for the Japanese people living in China.

In 1990, I had gone to Tokyo to be a TV producer. However, God had a different plan. During my first week there, I heard the gospel through a missionary. I accepted Jesus as my Savior, and my life changed. Every Sunday, I served at church as a simultaneous interpreter for the preacher.

As I studied in Japan and had the opportunity to set up a church in Japan, I realized that all of the Japanese corporations and companies in China would be a great target for churches in China. Beijing has about 10,000 Japanese people. It was great news that a Japanese church was going to be set up in Beijing for the first time. Together with four other Japanese missionaries, we planted the first Japanese church in Beijing. My job was to preach the Sunday sermon in Japanese once a month. We began with 20 people attending what was the first registered Japanese church in China's history.

At the same time, we continued to pray for and work toward reaching the Han Chinese (with a population of 1.2 billion), preparing to spread the gospel in large cities rather than country villages and to especially focus on intellectuals and the middle-class. Even though it is very important to preach the Gospel on a one-to-one basis, we trained the leaders of the home churches to help set up other new churches in different areas around China.

In the second month of our stay in Beijing, God gave me a huge task: to give a seminar to the 11 leaders of the home churches. The people living in the countryside and the country villages were filled with paganism and mysticism, so my goal was for the leaders to apply what they learned to their own lives.

OUR DAILY LIFE

Our lives were incredibly busy. We had to care for three young children: four-month-old Grace, four-year-old Dan, and five-year-old Segi. Every morning, my wife and I would send the two boys to kindergarten before going to language school. After four hours of classes, I would rush home to relieve my wife from childcare so that she could attend classes in the afternoon. For two hours every evening, we would do our homework with the help of our tutors. We took turns caring for the children as well as for each other.

In addition to church involvement, we made sure to have family worship every night, which was key in helping me maintain my spiritual well-being.

THE FIRST CHRISTMAS IN CHINA

During our first Christmas on the mission field, we were blessed with a number of gifts in different forms. Our first gift was a package from a Sunday school group at Kwang-sung Church in Korea. We were having dinner when the parcel was delivered; it seemed as if it had dropped from the heavens out of nowhere. The package was unexpected, so my family and I were all quite excited. "Wow!" "What is this?" "What could be in it?" "Come on, come on! Let's open it, quick!" We all raised our voices as we reached and grabbed for the package. I tried as much as possible to appear cool and calm, and said, "Let's all give thanks to God first," as I put my hands on the package. As soon as I finished the prayer, I ripped open the package in the same length of time it took for me to pray – about 2.5 seconds.

As I tried to separate my fingers from the sticky tape used to wrap the package, I looked into the box to see what had been delivered to us. My jaw dropped and it stayed down on the floor. There was a whole supermarket packed neatly in the box. It had Korean food, Korean hot chili paste, noodles, instant curry, toothpaste, crayons, pencils, storybooks, gloves, cookies, chewing gum, bubble gum, erasers, jump rope, masks, dolls, vitamin tablets, facial cream, and lotion. I just stood there and thought, "How in the world did they pack all that into this little box?" As we were reading the Christmas card sent with it, I remembered when I was in elementary school when I sent a gift and a letter to the military to encourage the men serving our country. Right then, I felt like we were soldiers of Christ serving on the front lines of the battle.

The encouragement and joy we received with the package meant so much to us, especially to my wife, who was suffering from an endemic skin disease. (She had been receiving treatment from the hospital, mostly antibiotic injections.) Also, it was a great joy to see Segi exclaiming, "This is so cool! God bless them!" He always wanted a jump-rope, sketch books and other children's story books.

Our second Christmas gift was less traditional, but just as important: an evangelistic gathering geared toward Japanese people. It had already been four months since the Japanese church had first been set up. On our first Christmas as a congregation, we had a unique experience. Ordinarily, in a seminar or gathering to reach out to the non-believers, the church members pray long and hard to prepare for that special occasion. However, for this gathering, it was the non-believers who were preparing long and hard to welcome the church members. This was unexplainable other than the fact that it was the work of God and that our prayers had been answered.

Here's the story behind it: In the capital of China, there are around 2,500 Japanese students studying abroad. Two hundred of these students were coming to a meeting once a month, and they asked us if they could participate in the Christmas events at our church. They wanted to know the true meaning of Christmas. They told us that they would provide the venue, the food, the stage equipment, lighting and everything that was needed for the event. We were to come along and sing hymns, give a sermon and have a Christmas service so that we could help them experience what Christmas should be all about. We told them that would be great if they would take care of the logistics, but in return we simply requested that drinking alcohol and smoking not be allowed during the event.

Our church had twenty members and we planned the whole event from beginning to end, praying for it to go well. We decided that the service should start by singing Japanese worship songs and be followed by a play based on Scripture. Then we would sing more songs of praise with our Korean worship group. After that, there would be a sermon, and then we would all light Christmas candles and pray for each other.

The whole event was carried out with all seriousness, and we were blessed to have the help of a worship group from a church in Korea. The Japanese students were deeply moved and after the service, told us things like, "We have experienced and heard a message loud and clear that could not have been heard elsewhere," "This is the first time in my life that I've had an amazing experience quite like this," "The worship, the songs of praise were so beautiful," and "I would like to visit the church sometime soon."

It was a meaningful Christmas event for both the church members and the Japanese students. However, none of the students came forward to say they wanted to believe in Jesus. The head of the group said, "It was a great and unique experience, and next year we will try our best to bring more people and prepare the event again so that we can invite you all and share Christmas together." All in all, the event, which God planned for us on that special day, turned out to be a successful bridge between the non-believers and the believers as we celebrated the birth of the Lord Jesus Christ.

The Christmas play during the event turned out to be a third Christmas gift to us, because of the wonderful participation of our three children. My daughter Grace was the leading actress in the play. She played the role of the baby Jesus. I know it sounds strange – a baby girl playing the role of baby Jesus – but we ran out of options because of the fact that there were no male babies around. Anyway, my daughter Grace hated the idea of being away from her mother and would cry every time we tried to rehearse. We prayed that she wouldn't cry when she played the role of baby Jesus, and our good Lord answered our prayers. I was so proud of the fact that she gave praise and glory to God even though she was just an infant. I was also proud of my sons, who played the role of the shepherds.

A fourth Christmas gift that year was seeing two people receive the gospel and come to Jesus. It had been four months since our arrival in Beijing, and I felt anxious to bring a lost soul to the Lord before the year ended. When I was in Japan, the United States and Korea, I evangelized to at least 10 people per year, and here I was – in the mission field – unable to evangelize to even one. Instead, I spent my time grumbling about the fact that I had to go to school and learn Chinese.

My struggles to master the language left me feeling hopeless, because I couldn't evangelize very well. And yet I was determined to master the language so that I could share the gospel. My desire to save souls and bring them to God was unwavering.

As soon as my wife and I arrived in China, we hired special tutors to teach us the Chinese language. Having a tutor in China was very cheap; almost everyone has a tutor to help them out. Our two tutors had been taking a course to get licensed to teach high school students and adults in their native language. They were the first locals to be in our home, so we prayed that they would be able to know God.

The two tutors were very helpful and kind, and also good teachers. They especially liked our children. We prayed for their salvation every single day and we told our kids to welcome the tutors with open hearts and arms whenever they stepped into our home. As time went by, they enjoyed our company more and more, and started to leave our house later than usual as our friendship got deeper. During this season, our Christmas event with the Japanese students was taking place, so my wife and I planned to give them a Bible as a Christmas gift and also invited them to the event. In China, it is illegal for a Chinese person to enter a foreign church, so it was a blessing that the venue was at a hotel. The tutors were really excited and curious what it would be like to be in a foreign Christmas event. The Christmas carol songs were sung and worship songs filled the hotel. Then the sermon was about to begin. The two tutors did not understand Japanese and their attention began to stray. I prayed to God and asked for wisdom as I tried to translate the message in broken Chinese.

The message that day was on "The Three Kinds of Love." The first kind is a love involving the question "What if?", the "If you would love me, I will love you with all my heart" kind of philosophy. The second kind of love is circumstantial love. When circumstances are all good and well, love can exist: You have no financial difficulties, you have a great job and it seems that you will be able to make me happy; therefore, I will love you. The third kind of love is unconditional love. This is the love that God gives us. True love is when someone sacrifices one's self. It is the kind of love that allows you to give yourself wholeheartedly to the person you love. God's love is like that. Jesus came from heaven to earth to prove that God's love is genuine. Therefore, Christmas is nothing without Christ. God sent His only Son as our Savior. Jesus restored our relationship with God by wiping our sins clean, making us white like snow.

After the sermon, I gave Bibles to the tutors and told them it was God's Word. They told me that they would read it. I thought that was it for the day, but my wife took it one step further. She shared what she had learned in her own quiet time with the Lord that morning. It was about Acts 26:1-23, when Paul told King Agrippa how his life was changed because of Jesus. He explained what his life was like before and after he met the Lord. Now, it was my wife's turn to explain how her life was changed before and after she met Jesus. Before becoming a Christian, her ambition was to have a successful career and make a lot of money. My wife confessed that she never had true happiness and peace in her life. She also said that after she believed in Jesus, her whole life was changed, her goals were realigned and she received true happiness and peace. This took about five minutes, but after she finished, the two tutors asked her immediately how to become a believer. She told them that through prayer they could talk with God and become a believer, and she offered to help them with that. Then they each said, "I would like to believe." My wife said, "Are you willing to accept Jesus into your life right at this moment?" They nodded and said, "Yes." My wife came to me and asked me to help with the prayer, and they sincerely accepted the Lord Jesus as their Savior.

After the prayer, I told them it was their spiritual birthday and that their souls had been reborn. I then gave them a little bit of advice about the Christian faith. It was truly a memorable moment for us since they were the first fruits that we had cultivated. My wife was even more overwhelmed by the situation. We just couldn't believe we evangelized anyone through our broken Chinese.

I remembered the story in Luke 5:17-20, when a few men carried a paralytic on a mat to take him to Jesus. One professor from the States asked a question to his students, "Who has led the paralytic to salvation?" Through this great experience, God gave me confidence that He works through men to achieve good. The two tutors continued to be spiritually on fire and were thirsty to read the Bible. They would read 20 chapters a night and come to my house with many questions that I would gladly answer. Our relationship strengthened and they helped us more with our learning the Chinese language.

Our fifth Christmas gift was the salvation of our housekeeper, Sauri. In China, missionaries use housekeepers in the homes partly for evangelistic purposes and partly to help with language difficulties. Sometimes they also help with the children, go to the grocery store and help with food preparation. Initially, Sauri helped us out for about two hours on Mondays, Wednesdays and Fridays. However, she had some problems while working with us. When she was using the vacuum cleaner, our daughter could not sleep and kept being woken up because of the loud noise. Security was another reason we had to let her go – we were uncomfortable with her having access to all the rooms in the house. We also felt it painted a poor picture of us as missionaries to have a housekeeper. While she was helping us out, I prayed daily for her salvation, but once she quit, it seemed hopeless to do so.

But since our two tutors came to Jesus, our mindset about Sauri changed. We prepared a gift for her and my wife called her and told her that we needed her help. She started working for us again the very next day. Soon after my wife was talking to Sauri and, once again, God used her as a tool to reach out to someone's soul. My wife translated the Four Spiritual Laws into Chinese with the help of our tutors. While my wife was preaching the gospel to Sauri, there was a moment of silence which was a bit awkward and felt uncomfortable since she didn't seem to be responding to the Gospel at all. Then my son Segi solved the problem simply by walking into the room and giving Sauri the Bible that my wife had wrapped in wrapping paper. He told her that it was a Christmas gift. Sauri smiled and opened the wrapping paper and said, "Someone was trying to preach to me before but I did not know how to believe in it." My wife explained the message of the gospel and Sauri decided to accept the Lord as her Savior. My wife and Sauri fell to their knees. My wife thanked God for the opportunity to share the gospel with Sauri and Sauri prayed for Jesus to come into her heart. As she was leaving, she asked my wife if she could get hold of another Bible so that she could give it to her mother when she visited her in January.

That was truly a blessing. We received the five wonderful gifts I mentioned here, along with many others. The most significant gift was, without a doubt, leading lost souls to Jesus. Without Christ Himself, Christmas doesn't mean a thing.

Sauri continued to study the Bible with my wife while also helping my wife out around the house. They would discuss what they had read the day before and shared it with one another. We realized the mission field truly was a place of harvest, where prepared workers could come out and evangelize. We were convinced that it was only the beginning of the wonderful work God had prepared for us.

OUR MINISTRY CONTINUES

Even though there was no one in China to "coach" us in what we were to do, we worked hard every single day to serve our Lord Jesus Christ. He said, "My Father is always at His work to this very day, and I, too, am working (John 5:17)." While serving in Beijing, we realized even more deeply what Jesus meant. '"My food," said Jesus, "is to do the will of Him who sent me and to finish his work... I tell you, open your eyes and look at the fields! They are ripe for harvest."' (John 4:34,35). These Scriptures explained exactly why our family was there: to carry out the mission we had been called to by our Lord, which was to evangelize the Chinese people.

God continued to open the door for us to reach out to other non-believers in China. We were able to evangelize six Han-Chinese, one Japanese and two Korean-Chinese; all of them committed their lives to Jesus Christ our Lord. My wife, with the help of our children, evangelized four of these people. With the guidance of the Holy Spirit, we started a Bible study group every Sunday evening. Six or seven people consistently attended these study groups, and their attitude towards learning became more and more serious. They would always arrive on time to the meetings, and after studying the Bible, they always wanted to stay a little bit longer to discuss the things they had learned.

We looked at Beijing as if it were a huge aquarium with many fish that were ready to be caught. If, in a missionary's eyes, the field he or she is in doesn't appear to have opportunities to spread the Gospel, they had better find a different field in which to evangelize. To be honest, I wanted to go and work in Ching-dao. However, we were advised to go to Beijing by our missionary organization. We thought that maybe God had a special plan for us to be carried out in Beijing. Our goals in our mission field were to set up a church in a city, to educate the leaders and to send out a missionary of our own. I think in God's eyes, it was appropriate for us to work in Beijing rather than Ching-dao. It could have been a good idea to evangelize to the people in Ching-dao; however, the population was limited to only the citizens of Ching-dao and San-dung. On the other hand, in Beijing, because of all the people from different parts of China, our targeted population was more diverse and could be more effective in reaching out to other people in other parts of China. The nine people who had accepted Christ so far were from nine different parts of China. These very people would be educated and prepared so that when they would go back to their hometowns, they would be able to preach to those they meet back at home. When I pictured this in my head, I could see the Word of God spreading all over the land of China. I saw this vision every time I looked at the huge map of China on the wall of my study.

God was at work, but, on the other hand, so was Satan, attacking the poor souls of China. Big and small accidents and illnesses attacked our fellow brothers and sisters. We ourselves suffered from frequent nightmares, headaches and stress, which made us very irritated and prevented us from doing our work. Our kids often had injuries. Satan set up many obstacles to prevent us from spreading the Good News.

WRITING THE NEXT CHAPTER OF ACTS

When you read a series of biographies written about missionaries, there is a certain feeling of awe that comes across your mind regarding the work of the Holy Spirit. Every time I have read these biographies, I think to myself, "I guess these things happened because it was during the early ages of missionary work...." or "I guess God chose these special people and used them as role models to change history."

I studied theology in the States. I vividly remember the last lecture of a professor who taught us the book of Acts. At the end of the lecture, the professor said, "The book of Acts is an uncompleted book. From now on, it is up to you to write the next chapters of Acts." I was extremely moved by that statement. When I look back, I realize that God was working through us to write the next chapters of the book of Acts.

Every Sunday afternoon, we had a Bible study group called "Open Heart, Open House (or the "Oh! Oh! Bible study")." Once, a local Christian couple visitedh our Bible study. The husband worked for a Japanese company in Beijing. They became Christians while studying at one of the top 10 universities in China. They were currently serving as leaders of a home church that had 40 members. It was the first time we ever had local Christians visit us, and it was exciting and nerve-wracking at the same time. We hadn't contacted any local Christians, other than those we reached out to evangelize, for security reasons.

After the Bible study, we had refreshments and asked the new visiting couple how they found out about the meeting. They told us that they knew of a young man who seemed to be troubled. Then, suddenly, he changed dramatically. His appearance was more presentable, he was kinder to people and seemed to be joyful all the time, as if he were a different person. They were curious and they asked him if something extremely good had happened to him. He told them that he had been attending a Bible study meeting that was taught by a Korean teacher who had come from the States and that he had learned many great things during the sessions. One day, something strange happened to the wife. She started to suffer from insomnia and felt constant fear, as if something was weighing her down. She was in so much pain that she asked God for help. Then God spoke to her and said, "Go and find the Korean Bible study teacher." That is how they got to our meeting. Listening to their story, I found it bizarre and was left speechless. That day, they asked me about several pastoral matters regarding their home church, and they went home with joy after receiving biblical answers from me. Their church was experiencing many problems. My wife and I prayed for them to have healthy, well-balanced spiritual growth, and for their church. They attended the next Bible study session looking healthy and joyful. We trained them for a year and now they are working and living in Tokyo, Japan.

THE FIRST BAPTISMS

During Easter that year, three of those to whom we had preached the gospel were baptized. I baptized them, firstly, as obedience on our part to Matthew 28:19-20, and secondly because of the fact that three others to whom we had preached the gospel previously had not come back from their hometowns during the national holidays. This was due to marriage problems, their parents holding them back, getting a new job, etc. If we had known beforehand that those people were not coming back, we would have baptized them, given them advice about keeping their faith, encouraged them in how to reach out to their families, relatives and friends, and also encouraged them to attend and serve in a church. There was no point regretting the things we didn't know or do, but after that, we decided that whenever we evangelized someone and they accepted Jesus Christ as their personal Savior, they would be baptized roughly three months later. Of course, during the three months, we would educate them about the basic tenets of Scripture and keeping the faith.

However, there were many problems that followed once we decided to baptize the born-again Christians: the place, the equipment, etc. Many prayer requests followed. We did not know what kind of a baptism God truly wanted. I prayed and waited and eventually God gave me an answer. I felt that God wanted me to teach the true meaning and the significance of baptism. I studied using many books related to baptism and prepared for the big event. I translated the material I had prepared and gave a lecture in the Chinese language.

The term "baptism" was very new to them and so it was hard for them to grasp the concept. They were having doubts and were thinking that because they already received salvation, they did not need to participate in this strange ritual. To help them understand, I told them a story about a religion in China that included a certain ritual that was called "baptism of fire." It was a very well-known and familiar ritual to the Chinese. I explained to them that trainees from many different parts of the country come and stay to be trained for months. They do not become disciples just by eating, drinking and being trained with their fellow trainees. They had to be baptized with fire, which would make a mark on their foreheads to symbolize the discipleship and make it official. They would then have an obligation and a responsibility to carry out their duties as a disciple. After I explained this, the new Christians understood the whole concept of "baptism" right away. I realized that knowing the culture and using it to explain certain Biblical concepts was a very effective strategy in preaching the gospel.

Being able to baptize those in the mission field was a very emotional experience for me, but, at the same time, it came with responsibility. If something went wrong, I would be responsible for everything and all of those who participated in the ceremony might be persecuted. Because of this, I reduced the number of people participating in the baptism, just in case something happened. On the day of the big event, only two people were invited other than the members of our meeting. One of the two was an elder who served as a leader in a Japanese church. The other was a 75-year-old-lady who had heard of the gospel from Hudson Taylor. She attended the event because her grandson was going to be baptized. The fascinating thing was that she seemed to be a walking Bible. While I was explaining about the baptism and mentioning certain Scriptures, this lady would just recite the Scriptures from memory, word for word.

Even though my Chinese language was not fluent, through God's grace, the ceremony was a success. After witnessing those who were baptized being joyful and happy and hearing their confessions of faith, I was able to feel the power of the gospel and God's own presence as He carried out His will among our generation.

The following is a confession of faith after the baptism of our brother Lee, who was the first to accept Jesus Christ as his Savior (among the three who were baptized that day):

Before I had faith, I had a vicious mind, full of greed, jealousy, arrogance and self-display. I was not able to distinguish right from wrong, I never did any good deeds and did not even think of trying to find God. I was continuing to live the path I have always walked on, without any hope, distancing myself from God. Then, one day, Jesus came and rescued me.

A person can die for someone who is his benefactor, but it is impossible to die for someone who is a complete stranger and has no relation to you. However, Jesus died for my sins, even though I was living a sinful life that I could not crawl out of. When I realized that God's love towards me was so great that He would give up His own Son to save me, I wanted to believe in Jesus.

The night of Christmas Eve 2005 was a very special and joyous night for me. It was the night I accepted Jesus Christ as my savior. There was a Christmas party that Mr. Shin invited us to. It took place at a hotel for Japanese students studying abroad. I went with a friend. Under the bright lights, I heard the Christmas carols and felt a great deal of peace in my heart in an atmosphere I had never been in before. The faces of people were full of joy; they were very kind and had gentle smiles on their faces. Then something happened in my heart; I had this urge to be like them. I wanted to be like them. I eventually gave in to this thought and went up to Mrs. Shin and said, "I want to believe in Jesus." Mr. and Mrs. Shin were very happy to hear me say this. They grabbed my hand and brought me to their friend who was able to translate for us. Their friend spoke Chinese and translated what the couple was saying. I read chapter 3 of the book of John. It was then I felt something I had never felt before. My mind seemed clearer without all of those worldly thoughts. I accepted Jesus Christ through prayer. As soon as I said the words, "I pray in Jesus' name, Amen" and opened my eyes, all of those people in front of me felt like brothers and sisters to me.

Today, Good Friday, on April 16, 2006, I proclaim that I am a Christian. I was baptized today. Today as I was being baptized I felt that the Holy Spirit was going to be with me forever. I am the not same person I was before. My external features are the same but my internal mindset is changed. There will be no more days where I will just waste my time doing something that is not important. I am going to reach out to those in need and I will make an effort to be kind to others. I will be happy when people are rejoicing; I will share sadness when others are sad. I will give up all my bad habits and behaviors and want to show God's love to others so that they too will be saved.

I have become one with Jesus through His love. No one can take this away from me. Even though hardships, persecution and destitution come my way, even though life-threatening situations will come across my path, I will not be afraid. Because I know that He will be there with me until the end of time.

SALVATION FOR AMY'S FAMILY

While we were studying at CIU in the States, our next door neighbors were a couple from China. They were studying theology. With our common love for the Chinese people, we became friends easily. Also, their son Joseph and our son Segi attended the same kindergarten. Amy's husband graduated from the university in his hometown and then received a doctorate from Michigan State University. He became a Christian after he had been working at a famous American car company — Chrysler. Then he decided to study theology at our university to become a missionary in China.

When we left the States, we made a promise to Amy and her husband to meet in China to work together as missionaries. About two years later, we received a letter from Amy; she wanted to visit us with her kids. The thought of a friend from the States visiting us was very exciting — as if we were waiting for reinforcements. She was the only friend to whom we could tell the secrets of our work in China.

The day Amy visited us, her older brother came along as well. He worked for the government in our state so was able to lead the way to our house. We were so pleased to see each other. Amy was surprised to see how fluent we were in the new language because two years ago, we couldn't even say a word. We were so happy to see each other that we didn't know what questions to ask, but because Amy's brother was there as well, we were not able to have a deeper conversation. Amy felt bad leaving early, so she invited us to her parents' house in the countryside and we promised that we would visit.

Amy's parents' house was so far away and up in the mountains that no taxi or bus could ever get to the place. We needed the help of Amy's older brother. He had an old car and took us to the mountains. The road was rough and we drove above a cliff. It seemed to be an endless trip. I asked him if we were there yet. He pointed his finger toward a cloud far away that covered the top of a mountain and said, "We need to go over that mountain in order to get to the house."

It took another hour to get to the mountain, and then we finally got to the little village up in the mountains where Amy's parents lived. Amy's older sister was taking care of her parents. It was very pleasant to see Amy again. They gave us a tour around their house. We came across a dark room, and I was startled because Amy's parents were sitting in the room without any lights on. It was a little strange, but I made an effort to smile and said hello. When they saw our one-year-old daughter, Grace, their faces lit up. Because of our daughter, we were also able to become close to the other relatives very quickly.

My wife talked to them about Jesus. Amy's father, who was 85 years old, kept asking the same question: "Who is Jesus? Who is he?" Amy's father said he had lived in the village for decades, but he had never heard of Jesus before. Because transportation to and from the village was very difficult, the village was rarely visited by anyone – the road to the village had been made only two years ago. I realized that we were the first Christians ever to have preached the gospel to these villagers since Jesus came to save us 2006 years ago. We felt very proud and very burdened to preach the gospel.

The Holy Spirit again used my wife first. She had many fears, but had changed to become a professional "fisherman" to bring people to Jesus. My wife went to Amy's mother and said, "I am a Korean who has come from America. I have left my family and come here, but I have joy and peace in my life. When we have to go to a different country, we need a plane ticket to get there, when we have to go on a vacation or a holiday, we need a train ticket. When we die, there is Heaven and Hell, but to get to Heaven, we need a 'Jesus ticket' …" My wife started to evangelize Amy's parents while I was teaching Amy effective ways to preach the gospel to one's family and relatives.

Amy had been busy taking care of the household, the children and her husband, so she never had the opportunity during her 13-year stay in the States to preach the gospel to her family. But the number one priority on her prayer request list was the salvation of her family. Even though my language was not fluent, she understood what I was explaining to her. After about an hour of me lecturing on how to preach the gospel to your families and relatives, my wife came to me and said that Amy's parents wanted to believe in Jesus and that they wanted to know more about Him. When Amy heard this, she stood up, picked up a pen and a large calendar and took her parents into their room. Her father had a hearing problem and her mother was a little blind. Amy started to preach in a loud voice while writing on the back of the calendar in big block Chinese letters.

While Amy was preaching, her older sister was also interested and was listening carefully to what her sister was explaining to their parents. As a result, Amy's sister wanted to become a Christian and my wife helped her with the prayer. Amy's older brother, who was listening from outside, thought it was all interesting and he also became a Christian and accepted Jesus as His personal savior. Eventually, that night, Amy's parents, her brother and sister became believers of Christ. Amy's older sister's kids were also there, but they were too young to understand the gospel that they had just heard. So we prayed for them, that someday they too would know Jesus. The next day, we gave them a few suggestions and had a few more pleasant conversations and left to go back home.

This particular trip was very significant. We had been putting together a strategy that basically said, "Preaching the gospel will be most successful by training a Chinese person so that he/she may preach the gospel to their fellow Chinese people." This trip was like putting that theory and strategy into practice. It was very exciting to see it in action! Through this experience, we were able to learn a few things to help spread the Gospel more effectively and were also reminded that the Holy Spirit was in charge of all of these great things that were happening.

When we look back, we now realize that all of this was part of God's great plan. The fact that Amy moved right next door to our house when we lived in the States and every single thing that had happened since then was all of the work of the Holy Spirit. Amy's prayer request was answered. God poured his blessing on Amy's family more than they could have ever imagined.

However, one downside of this journey was that our three kids got really ill after we came back. They were suffering from severe coughing and diarrhea. We later found out that it was because of the water that they drank in the mountains. Our youngest child, Grace, could not eat anything for four days and became weak and thin like the kids you see on television who are dying from poverty and illness. Looking at our poor little Grace lying on her bed made me think about all of the hardships that our predecessors who preached the Gospel had to face for many years.

Even now, God is looking for authors to keep running the marathon of completing the Great Commission; to write the next chapters of the book of Acts. The Holy Spirit has the power to write it and complete it Himself, but He is waiting for more workers so that we can all contribute to God's great plan.

OUR FIRST CHINESE BIBLE STUDY

Somehow, I ended up leading a Bible study group without a translator in the tenth month that we were in China. A brother who used to translate for us was ill, so it was left up to me to lead the study group without a translator. At first, it was very nerve-wracking for me and I had no confidence at all. However, God helped me and the brothers and sisters encouraged me to lead the study group. Because of the short time I had to prepare, the actual time it took for the Bible study became much shorter and the lecture itself was short, precise and to the point. It also became a group discussion, with questions and answers, rather than just me talking the whole time and everyone else sitting and listening. Because of this, the participants became more involved and had more opportunities to share their thoughts, which enabled me to understand them a little bit more and help them with their spiritual growth. After three months, the study group became very active and conversational, even without the translation. It wasn't because I was fluent in speaking the language – it was by God's grace that I was able to teach my brothers and sisters in Christ.

VISITING A HOME CHURCH FOR THE FIRST TIME

We had an opportunity to visit a home church for the first time since we had arrived in China. We had had a few conversations and meetings with the leaders of the home churches, but it was the first time that we actually participated in a service in a home church. There were 20 or so brothers and sisters who welcomed us. There were quite a few questions that were asked, but because of security reasons, we were not able to answer all of them. As a result, our conversations were limited in depth.

That same day, we were introduced to four female university students who were there to help with the church. Unlike what I had imagined, they were extremely dynamic, emotional and genuinely interested in the missionary work that was being done. I went from being a quiet visitor to having long conversations with the students. I told them about the importance of being able to serve others through the Bible, the training programs they needed to have, the importance of studying theology, having a mentor and someone as a supporter, being able to be flexible in the mission field, the salvation of their own families and the importance of marriage.

As it was getting late and we were trying to go back home, one of the members of the home church came up to me, holding the Bible and reading a verse. It was Hebrews 12:1, which says, "Therefore, since we are surrounded by such a great cloud of witnesses." When he read this verse, he told us, "You are these very men."

THE BIRTH OF JAO-YANG CHURCH

Our "Oh! Oh!" Bible study group increased in numbers; there were soon 16 members, including children. One of our members had volunteered her house to be used for our own worship services. Of course, there were many suggestions within our study group that we should start our own home church; however, our family had just arrived and I did not think that the other members of the group were ready to be the foundation of a church.

We started to pray, decided on a name for the home church and determined each of our roles in the home church. When we all meet in Heaven, we will remember the day we started the church as a significant day, and we will be praised by God and receive rewards. However, on that day, we ended the discussion for starting a new home church with tension, fear and a feeling of expectancy. We decided to use the initials of the church location for its name and I suggested adding "The Word" into the name to remind us to live our lives according to the Word of God.

The first service in honor of our new church was at our beloved sister Zhao's house. Her house was very clean and simple, as if she had prepared her house to be a place where worship services would take place. There was also a piano, since she was a piano teacher. We didn't have a bulletin or handout of what hymns would be sung or what Bible verses would be read;

we just had a simple worship service. However, it turned out to be a much more spiritual, joyful and exciting time than we had expected. We could feel God's presence among us. The sermon I preached was from Genesis 12:1-3, about how we could be a blessing to others in China just as our sister Zhao was being a blessing by providing her home.

That, unfortunately, was the only time we had our service at sister Zhao's home. Due to strong opposition from her boyfriend, we had to move our church to our home.

THE FIRST EVANGELICAL TRIP

After the home church was set up, we had our first outdoor worship service. To be more precise, it was more like the beginning of an evangelistic journey, rather than a worship service. We were planning effective strategies while we were on our journey to preach the gospel to the people of China. Anyone who was interested in Christianity was welcomed to join us on our little trip. It had been awhile since we were outside of the city, so we were all happy for a change of scenery. It is easy to forget the everyday things, and become more relaxed and straightforward when you see things from a different perspective, which ended up positively affecting our efforts to preach the gospel.

During our trip, my wife and I were having conversations with the other people who were traveling with us. Since we were foreigners, there were many interesting topics that came out of the conversations. As we spoke, the Holy Spirit gave us courage to talk about the gospel. At that exact time that we spoke of the gospel as the Holy Spirit instructed us to do, He came into their lives and they received salvation. After they dedicated their lives to Jesus, we told everyone else around us, as witnesses, so that they would remain committed. Then, just before we moved on to the next person, we would ask the driver to stop for a while at a public toilet so that we could have a short break. When we got back on the bus again, we would deliberately sit next to a different person so that we might share the gospel with them.

One of the four Han people who were invited on this trip was a 27-year-old young man named Yang. When I shared the Gospel with him, he received our Lord Jesus Christ as his personal savior. The other three people promised me that they would come to the home church and study the Bible every week. Before Yang had received Jesus Christ and before he prayed, he told me, "When you said 'Forgiveness is making a decision,' in your sermon today, it was very powerful." Then he told me that he had decided to believe in Jesus Christ. He also told me that although he often went on business trips, on the days when he was home, he would attend our home church. If he had to go on a business trip, he would ask me for homework so that he would study the Bible while he was away. God uses people like him who have a pure and genuine heart.

After a two-hour bus ride, we arrived at a famous tourist attraction. One thing that was very surprising was that many of those who were traveling with us told me that they had never been there before. Because of this, they were extremely happy to be there. God truly provided us with an amazing place for us to remember our first church outing as Jao-Yang Church members.

OUR SECOND CHRISTMAS IN CHINA

For our second Christmas in China, the Lord once again gave us a multitude of gifts. The first was when God brilliantly answered our longtime prayer request for Jao-Yang Church. We had been having the worship and prayer meetings at our house for over a year and it had become quite uncomfortable for my wife and children. The kids had to stay quiet for many hours until the meeting was over and my wife had to clean the house, prepare the food, and wash an enormous amount of dishes. Eventually, the stress was too much for our family, but even if we could find a place where we could worship, trying to rent another place was financially difficult. Continuing with the worship services at our house became even more difficult as our membership grew in number. A place where we could worship was our biggest prayer request.

But God solved our problem in a way that was beyond our imagination. One of the members, a young Japanese woman called Naomi was thinking of starting up a new business. She suggested having our worship services at her office. Of course, a little bit of a rental fee was needed to use the place, but that wasn't a big problem. The office was at a perfect location for us to meet. It was a simple, rectangular apartment that was suitable for a worship service. Also, the place was under her name, so it was a safe place to have a Sunday worship service. We had our first Christmas together as a fellowship at our new location. We were truly thankful that we were able to put a small cross on one wall and thanked God that He provided a great place for us to worship Him.

Our second gift was the baptism of two people during Christmas break. One of them was a lady whom we had first evangelized. She worked as a private teacher and became a Christian when she heard the gospel from us. The other young lady who was baptized had majored in dance at the university and was then working at Samsung. She had come to Christ through our group Bible study.

Our third Christmas gift was similar to one we had a year before: another surprising and miraculous Christmas gathering at the Japanese church. Usually, for an evangelistic gathering, the church works hard to invite nonbelievers to church. However, with the power of the Holy Spirit, the exact opposite had happened. The Japanese students living in Beijing invited our church members to their meeting so that we could have a joint Christmas gathering. The purpose of the gathering was to learn about the true meaning of Christmas and experience what it was like to be in a Christmas worship service. One hundred and thirty Japanese students attended this special gathering. If this exact meeting had occurred in Japan, with 130 young students attending a worship service for more than an hour, it would have been considered a miracle. However, it occurred in our city. Only by the power of the Holy Spirit could such a miraculous event have occurred. These students did not carry cigarettes or alcohol with them at the church's request. Members of the Korean congregation, the French church and the American church served as the praise team, and I served as the translator. Unfortunately, no one was converted to Christ that night, but we were not discouraged or disappointed, because we knew that God had reached out to their hearts.

Our fourth Christmas gift occurred at the Christmas parties we had with the Jao-Yang Church members in two different places. One took place within the new church building; the other was at our house. When we gathered at our house, we were full of joy as we ate the food that my wife had prepared. On that special night, a lady from the Han race named Chen came to Christ. When she committed her life to Christ, she told us that she had never been in such a joyful atmosphere in her entire life.

A week later, we had another Christmas party and Chen brought a friend with her. I had the privilege of introducing our Lord Jesus Christ to Chen's friend. She had a few questions about Christianity and God, and then accepted Jesus Christ as her savior. We found out a few moments later that these two ladies were roommates.

Many of the plans that I had made and prayed about for a long time had been answered. I was excited to see how God would continue to work.

Interestingly enough, we received our fifth Christmas gift while giving gifts to others. We had decided during our Christmas break that our church would provide Christmas gifts to our neighbors living in poverty. Through this experience, we also wanted to teach our church members how contributions would be used as donations. The Holy Spirit gave this wonderful idea to my wife while she was praying and became a reality through my business experience. There were many young men and women who came to the city to work for a cleaning company. These young men and women worked 10 hours a day, without a single day off, and got paid roughly the equivalent of 95 U.S. dollars per month. Our fellow missionaries contributed to our church so that we could buy presents for these young men and women.

My wife called the cleaning company and found out that there were 60 people working for them. When my wife told them that our church wanted to send them Christmas presents, the loud yells and shouts could be heard from our end of the telephone. We prepared 60 Christmas presents, which included gloves, socks, fruits, sweets, chips, moon pies and Christmas cards.

On Christmas Eve, some of our church members decided to visit the cleaning company, so we went and had a great time meeting the young men and women. A lady from our church briefly told the employees about our church and who we were and that we would love to share Christmas with them. We also introduced ourselves as Christians and told them that if anyone had any questions, we would be glad to answer them. Then a young lady came forward and courageously told us that she was a Christian, which is not an easy thing to do, and began explaining Christianity in more detail. It seemed to us that God had already put one of His chosen people within that crowd in advance. At first, people were a bit shy and afraid to come forward, but later they were full of joy and thanked us for the presents and for visiting them. Through the joyful faces of these young men and women, I was able to experience the presence of our Lord. It seemed that He also had a warm smile on His face.

Our sixth Christmas gift came in the form of an opportunity I had to deliver a lecture on the book of Revelation. The audience was 18 young college students (Han Chinese). I had been researching Revelation in depth while I was studying in the United States. I was able to learn much while I had been staying at the home of a professor named Pil-chan Lee, who had specialized in the book of Revelation. During his sabbatical year he lent us his house so our family could live in it. I read his books on Revelation, which included different translations, and became more familiar with the analytical research. Also, the fact that I had given a lecture on the book of Daniel the year before was a helpful experience. Through this lecture, I found the correct perspective in looking at the book of Revelation. It was a great joy and privilege for me to go through this experience.

The Bible can be approached from different angles. In the perspective of relationships, the Old Testament can be summarized as the relationship between God and His chosen people, while the New Testament can be summarized as the relationship between Christ and His church. The Book of Revelations is about the relationship between our Lord as the Judge, the Lamb, the Bridegroom and His Church, as the Bride. When one considers the "relationships" that occur in the Bible in depth, the Old Testament is focused on the relationship between the master and the servant, and the law. The New Testament, on the other hand, focuses on the more spontaneous horizontal relationship between friends. The book of Revelation goes a step further and describes the relationship as the more intimate one of a married couple. Therefore, the Bible can be summarized as a book that focuses on the relationship between God and His chosen people as well as the relationship between our Lord Jesus Christ and His church. The book of Revelation is a unique book of the Bible, as it promises special blessings for those who research and study it (Revelation 1:3), but it also promises to curse those who add to or subtract from the Word of God (Revelations 22:18,19). Going through this process of readjustment of my understanding of the Bible was a great Christmas gift from God.

Our last Christmas gift was a book I read called *Laying It All Down*, which was written by a man named Young-gyu Lee, a missionary in Mongolia. He wrote, "God's first initial notion is not transformation of the people being reached out to, but the missionary's own transformation. The most important work that a missionary needs to have the focus on, is by following our Lord's character. Through the process of the transformation, God's kingdom will expand on the land in which the missionary has set foot on." (Young-gyu Lee 191, 2006)

GOD MAKES EVERYTHING POSSIBLE

The church in China is much like the early church in Acts. The tremendous work of the Holy Spirit for building His churches is endless, so our daily life is full of wonderful and amazing events.

My wife and I came to a realization of something extremely important. As Christians, one of the most fundamental beliefs is that everything that we do is not something we do ourselves, but that God does in our lives. We realized that we needed to work hard as if we were doing everything ourselves, but that in reality, God was working through us and making everything possible. God will carry out His will no matter what, even by using other people; He doesn't have to use us. It is by God's grace that He uses us in a certain time and place.

When we considered the amount of prayer and effort carried out by many people so that one soul would receive salvation, we realized that we were playing such a small role. Of course, there were a few Chinese people who had received the gospel through us; they had never heard the gospel before. When I look back, I wonder, if they had been preached to by other Christians who were more faithful, would they have been under better care?

A PHONE CALL FROM A FRIEND

The telephone rang one morning in May. Most of the phone calls that came early in the morning usually came from the States. Just as I assumed, the phone call was from my Chinese friend Amy. She told me that her nephew (the son of her older sister) had gone through two surgeries because of his brain cancer. Amy told me that there was not much hope and wanted me to share the gospel with him before it was too late. My wife and I fasted and prayed for Amy's nephew. The next morning, I met Amy's older brother and went to her sister's house. It took an hour-and-a-half of driving along the highway before we arrived at a small city apartment. When Amy had told me about her nephew, I assumed he would be a teenager, but to my surprise, he was a 40-year-old man. Her older sister was over 60 years old. As we arrived at her house, their family came out and greeted us. I told her that I was a Christian, that her sister Amy was also a believer and that I was there to share the gospel. I asked them if they wanted to hear about Jesus and they were glad to do so. I handed out something I had prepared beforehand through prayer. They read the sheets I had prepared about the gospel and about God's "genuine blessing." They became more curious and interested about the gospel. Amy's brother-in-law, who was also more than 60 years old, told me that he had heard of the gospel 45 years ago, but that this was the first time he had heard of the gospel since then.

I began preaching the gospel through the book of Mark; specifically, through the story of the lady who had been subject to bleeding for twelve years (Mark 5:25-33). In Mark 5:26, it says, "She had suffered a great deal under the care of many doctors and had spent all she had, yet instead of getting better she grew worse." It was during this most dreadful and hopeless situation that the lady heard about Jesus. After I had explained the story up to this point, I looked at Amy's nephew and I told him that the story of the lady written in the Bible was quite similar to the situation he was in. As soon as I said this, his eyes lit up and he showed great concern and curiosity. I told him that he had also heard of Jesus, just like this lady, but the difference was that she received Jesus as her personal savior and was cured. Jesus told the woman in Mark 5:34, "Daughter, your faith has healed you. Go in peace and be freed from your suffering." I told the nephew, "This very faith is what you need right now. I want to share more about Jesus so that you may have more faith in Him. Would you like to hear more about Him?" As soon as I asked them this question, all three of them said "Yes." I introduced our Lord Jesus Christ and shared the gospel with them.

When they heard of the gospel, they all told me that they wanted to believe in Jesus. We all held hands and prayed together. I prayed once more for the nephew who had been fighting brain cancer for a long time. After the prayer, I told them that they had been spiritually re-born and therefore it was crucial that they grow and mature spiritually. I gave them a few suggestions on how to achieve this.

Before we left, I asked the couple what kind of work they did when they were younger. They told me that they both had been middle school teachers. They had both retired and were now staying at home. I was wondering at how easily and how well they understood the gospel when I was preaching it to them. I then asked what kind of work their son did before he became ill. The father smiled and replied that he was a police officer. In China, missionaries are most afraid of government officials and police officers. It is quite funny in the sense that God gave me an opportunity to share the gospel with a police officer and that he came to believe in God.

Now, I did not know that there was a church in this small city. They told us that they hadn't seen a church building within the city; however, they had seen a church being built downtown. So I advised the family that until the church was built, the family should have worship services within the house. I gave them a few tips on how to have worship services at home. I requested that they share the gospel with their relatives, friends and neighbors. They told me time and time again that the next time I visited them, it should be with my whole family.

ANOTHER EVANGELISM TRIP

Our church decided to go on an evangelism trip to a place in Beijing where they had natural caves. We told our church members to invite people to this special trip, but only one person brought their friend. I asked the others how come they hadn't brought anyone with them, and they told me that they weren't able to find anyone who they could bring. I smiled and replied, "There are 1.3 billion people living in China, and you're telling me that there is no one to bring?" The church members nodded and laughed. Our new member who had joined us was a brother named Lee Jin, an architect. I thought to myself that this trip must have been made for this special brother and sat next to him when I got on the bus. I asked him if he had heard of Jesus before. As soon as I asked him this question, he began to lecture me. Apparently, he had been approached by five different people who were trying to share the gospel with him. He said that everyone has their own opinions and is entitled to have their own beliefs; therefore, no one should force anyone to convert to a religion. He said he planned to watch and observe many people from many different religions so that he would be able to make a final decision as to what religion he would chose to believe when he got older. I think he felt quite sorry that he had spoken for such a long time, and so he added to his conclusion that despite all of this, he thought Jesus had done the most good deeds and was the most admirable and respectable founder of a religion than any other leaders or founders of other religions.

I thought to myself, "Now, I have finally met my match." I don't recall meeting anyone quite like him before. I suddenly felt really tired and did not have the confidence to share the gospel with him. So I prayed silently and said to God, "I will obey your command and I will speak of the gospel to the very best of my abilities. The next step is your turn. You take care of the rest." Then I told the brother, "You seem to know quite a bit about Christianity, but there are some aspects that you seem to have misunderstood. If you would like, I would like to explain in detail, about God the Creator, about Jesus, and about the Bible itself. How about it?" Then I added, "After you have listened to my explanation, it is up to you to believe or not to believe in the things I have shared with you. Are you willing to do that?" With delight he said, "I like the way in which you approached me with your kindness and hospitality. Other people always say, 'It is great to believe in Jesus. You must also believe!' They always force people to go to church. It was quite irritating and intolerable the way they approached me. But you, on the other hand, don't seem to put pressure on me and make me want to listen to you. OK. I want to hear about it." It was then I had a gut feeling that today this brother would receive salvation.

I made him read the first chapter of Genesis and explained to him the important aspects of the chapter. God first provided an environment that humans can live in, then He created man and made him to be the manager and administrator of the things He had created. Therefore, it is wrong for a human being to worship other creatures, whether it is a large tree or a high mountain or strong animals. Because Lee Jin was an interior architect, I tried to explain it from his perspective. I told him it was like how after finding a suitable home and decorating the interior, all you then need to do is to go in and live in the house. He found it interesting and understood what I was getting at.

After he read chapter 2, I explained that God made man out of dirt and breathed life into the nostrils. That is why when people die, we turn back into dirt. This definitely shows that humans were once dirt themselves and proves that the words written in the Bible are correct. He told me that that seemed to make sense. I told him, "But the problem is, our spirit needs to go back where it came from. God made two places; heaven and hell. If you are not qualified to enter heaven, you will have no choice but go to hell. This is just like the way the Chinese government puts criminals into jail. We can't complain why someone made this sort of system." He agreed with the example I gave. I continued. "Just like a criminal must go to prison even though he doesn't want to, sinners must go to a spiritual prison called hell." He was surprised to hear this and wanted to listen more and more about it, and through the work of the Holy Spirit, his curiosity seemed to grow.

While reading chapter 3 of Genesis, I explained to him the first sin that man ever committed, the sin of disobedience. I explained that God hates sin. Because of sin, the relationship between man and God became bad, because back then there were no written books and people seemed to forget who their Creator was. When I explained all of this to Lee Jin, he seemed to understand and kept nodding his head.

After I had explained to him more of the gospel, I asked him if he understood the things I had explained to him so far. He replied, "Yes." I asked him, "Do you want to believe in Jesus, the Savior who has died for your sins instead of you?" He replied, "I will go home, read the Bible more, think a little more, observe other Christians' lives, and when I feel that I want to believe, then I will come to you and tell you that I would want to believe in Jesus."

The most difficult thing when sharing the gospel with someone is trying to evangelize a person who has already made up his or her mind, and who knows the answer and the perfect timing to reject the gospel (especially the Japanese people). He seemed to believe that if he rejected in a polite way, then I would have no choice but to back away and he would be able to "escape" the conversation. I bet he had used this method on a couple of other people, too. I knew it was the Holy Spirit's turn to work. I boldly opened my mouth. I told him that when you need to go to a foreign country, you need a visa. After you have received the visa, you need to prepare a few things. If you don't receive the visa, you cannot go anywhere abroad. You need to receive a visa from heaven when you want to go to heaven. You first need to receive a visa named "Jesus" and then think about how you will live your life. When Lee Jin heard this, his eyes were filled with light and his face became brighter. He said, "That is right. I understand it now. Yep. I will first believe in Jesus." I was so encouraged by this and told him, "When a baby is born, he does not know his own name, the address of his house, his parents' names and doesn't know anything about life itself. However, one thing is for certain, that he is a human being created in the image of God, and that he needs to be born into this earth in order to figure it all out. When he is born, then, he is able to think about how he will live his life, the question of being a person that will be respected and deemed worthy by God. That is the question that he needs to consider after he is born." Lee Jin told me that he understood and that he wanted to believe in Jesus.

After we held hands together and prayed, the bus arrived at our destination. I told him about the healthy new life he was about to live, now that he had been spiritually reborn in Christ. I gave him some advice on the things he needed to do. I told the church members that our brother Lee Jin had just accepted our Lord Jesus Christ as his personal savior. Every single member of our church gave a loud cheer and truly blessed Lee Jin.

When we arrived at the cave, we walked for two kilometers underground and then came upon a big lake. There were a few small ferryboats that were carrying people around. Roughly eight people could get on board each boat, and it was really uncomfortable. We had to squeeze everybody on board. The ferryman was a lady and she started to recite a poem she wrote. I thought to myself, "What can she be so excited and joyful about? She is working in a dark, lonesome place, in a cave of all places? There is something unique about this woman." Then, to my surprise, she told us that God had created a mysterious and marvelous place such as this, so that we may enjoy it. One of the brothers who came along with us asked her "Excuse me, are you a Christian by any chance?" She replied with a loud and clear voice, "Wo shi Jidutu" (I am a Christian). I was so surprised and happy and told her that all of us on board were Christians as well. She was also amazed and said, "Really?! Let us sing a song of praise!" and she began to sing. Unfortunately, we were not able to sing along with her, as the song she sang was an old hymn. When she had finished her song of praise, we sang a gospel song that we knew. Beautiful voices of praise were echoing throughout the quiet cave. Without any hindrance, a perfect harmony of sound filled the atmosphere within the cave God had created for us.

Then she suddenly told us to turn off our cameras and anything with light shining. I remembered the time while I was in a cave in Tennessee and was expecting to see something miraculous. When it was pitch black, she lifted the Lord's name on high and blessed us with her prayer. It was so moving. It was as if we were witnessing a modern-day John the Baptist, preaching the Word of God in the lowest part of Beijing, underground, with a 300-meter-long lake as her mission field. She continued and said, "I have received so many things from God that I cannot even remember, but I haven't returned to Him as much as I should. I have been given numerous things from God, but I gave so little." She said that she earned 8 Wien (a little over $1) per day while working down in the caves. That was the lowest daily salary I had ever heard since I arrived in Beijing. She believed in Jesus when she was 18 years old and now she was 43. She said that God sent her there, and she looked truly happy. We received God's grace through her as we walked four kilometers further into the cave. At first we were wondering and complaining why we needed to walk so far, but then we realized that God planned something beforehand in arranging this special meeting with her. We received much encouragement and much grace from God.

A YOUNG MAN NAMED JIN DONG

There was a young man named Jin Dong in our church. He always seemed alone and depressed. His hometown was a place called Sandong, and he had became a believer through a Korean missionary six years earlier. He was looking for a job in Beijing when we first met. We came to realize a few things after getting to know him for over a year: He was extremely introverted, he wasn't able to take care of himself, he had Confucian beliefs, and he had a superior attitude about China and a very narrow-minded way of looking at things. He was 29 years old, a college graduate, but the one thing that stood out about him was that he was never able to give thanks for or appreciate anything in his life. Either he wasn't expressing it, or he wasn't appreciating anything.

The many things I couldn't understand about this young man were always in the back of my mind and the focus of my prayers. One day in particular I started praying for him, and every time I started to pray, the Holy Spirit reminded me of something. When Jin Dong smiled, it exposed his toothless mouth. It is as if there were a hole in his mouth, and it must have been stressful for him.

One day, my wife and I went to the dentist. In Beijing, the water is so bad that teeth get damaged easily and quickly. Apparently the dentist was a well-known Korean doctor. He asked me if I was a missionary. Over here, that is a question that shouldn't be asked because of security. When he noticed that I was startled by the question, he kindly introduced himself. He said he was a deacon at a Korean church in Beijing and told me that many missionaries come to his hospital. He also added that he had an interest in missionary work involving medical care. I suddenly remembered Jin Dong's teeth and told the dentist about him. I asked him if he would be able to treat him. The dentist was glad to help and said, "Bring him over here sometime. Don't worry about the fees; I will take care of it." It was truly amazing. I couldn't believe the generosity of this Christian man. It was totally a "Hallelujah" moment. A few days later, I took Jin Dong to the dentist. The dentist looked at his teeth and told him, "You are 29 years old, and yet your teeth are those of a 70 year old man's." He showed Jin Dong eight broken and rotten teeth from his mouth. The rest of the teeth didn't seem to be healthy either. The dentist asked him, "How on earth have you taken care of your teeth?" The dentist said that it would take around two months to fix the problems and that the treatment would be quite expensive. When I heard this, I felt extremely sorry for the dentist. I asked him, "Can I help you out with the fee?" The dentist said, "No, no, no. Don't worry about it. I will take care of everything."

About two months later, when the treatment was complete, Jin Dong sent me a text message. He said, "I thank God for all the things you have done for me." It was the first "Thank you" I had heard from him. Just like someone blames his or her parents for a part of their body that they are not happy with, Jin Dong had an inferiority complex that made him forget the many things that he should be thankful for. My wife and I were so moved by the transformation that had occurred in Jin Dong life and thanked God for providing this opportunity to glorify His name. We invited the dentist and his wife over to our house for dinner on behalf of Jin Dong and thanked him over and over again.

Soon after, I got call from Jin Dong. He said his brother was going to come to Beijing, and he wanted to meet us. I believed it to be an indication that he needed my help to share the gospel with his brother. Since my wife was not at home, I prepared some food and drink to serve them.

Jin Dong's brother was 39 years old and good-looking. His personality was also very different from Jin Dong's. He first said to me, "Thanks for taking care of my brother," in a very polite way. I said, "God loves your brother so much. God prepared a great dentist for your brother. So don't thank me." Then, I asked him whether his hometown had any church. He said there were about six churches in his hometown. I was quietly surprised, and asked him if he had ever been to church. He said "not even once." I asked him whether he had ever heard about Jesus or not. He said he had heard about him but didn't know much. I asked him, "Is it okay with you if I tell you about Jesus and church?" He said okay. It seemed like he had a good impression of Christianity since the Christian dentist had cured his brother for free.

I told him the good news with my experimental method. First, I had him read the first three chapters of Genesis. I began to explain the main points using facets of Chinese culture so as to help him understand. Hearing my explanation, his worldview began to break down. He showed great interest in my explanation. I used the example of a bridge to explain the good news. Specifically, I explained who Jesus is, what He has done and what accepting Jesus means. Finally, I made him read Romans 10:9,13. He hesitated. "I sort of understand, but I haven't properly read the Bible yet, so I don't know whether I should believe Jesus or not." I took him to John 1:12 and showed him what it means to believe in Jesus. I said, "Believing in Jesus makes you a child of God. So far, your life has been driven by you; however, if you accept God's Son Jesus, God will guide you and protect you because you are His child." Eventually, he resolutely and loudly answered, "I will believe in Jesus." At last, we held hands together and prayed. I gave him some suggestions for healthy spiritual growth. Afterward, he said, "My hometown is famous for its rice. After harvest, I will bring some rice and visit you one more time." He was excited. I could see that his features were completely different. He left our home with a Bible in his hands.

After three months, Jin Dong was finally finished with his dental surgery. One day, I asked him whether he had written a thank you letter to doctor. He said he hadn't. It made me a bit angry. I had already told him so many times to write a letter, and it had been a month since the surgery at this point. He was thirty years old — unless he was a child, he should have expressed his gratitude to the doctor. I absolutely couldn't understand. However, I restrained myself and told him one more time that Christians should be thankful for even small things.

A few days later, my wife was washing rice for cooking and said, "I don't get how quickly we used up all this rice. In America, we didn't worry about rice, because God sent us enough rice through deaconess Park E Boon and Kim Myung-hye every month. However, in China, since we serve so many people, we often lack rice. God help us!" After hearing her speak, I thought in my heart that God wouldn't answer her prayer. In America, we didn't have any income, so God had provided us rice through other people. However, in Beijing, we received sponsorship every month, so we could use our own money to buy it. However, contrary to my expectation, my wife got a surprising answer to her prayer the following week.

After three days, Jin Dong left me a message saying his brother was coming with packs of rice. Three months before, when Jin Dong's brother told me he would bring us rice, I assumed it was just a courteous statement. I was astonished and thought it would be good to buy Jin Dong's brother's rice, because we needed rice anyway. Above all, I was curious about how he was keeping the faith. I was excited that I could meet him again and praise the Lord with him. The next day, I got a call from Jin Dong's brother saying that he had just now arrived in Beijing. I wanted to send my car to pick him up, but he said that would be inconvenient for me. So he called a delivery car to bring the rice to my home. I worried it may cost him a lot of money, but I couldn't do anything but wait.

Jin Dong called me again when he and his brother arrived at my apartment. I went downstairs to see them. Surprisingly, Jin Dong's brother had brought 20 packages of rice (equivalent to 200 kilograms of rice), two packs of flavored rice, two boxes of duck eggs, two packs of glutinous rice, two packs of red beans, a bag of special beans, and two packs of wild rice. Of course I was amazed, but at the same time, I worried about how I would pay for all of it.

I first gave them some refreshment, and asked how Jin Dong had been. Then, I carefully asked, "How much did you bring? I want to pay for them." Jin Dong's brother said, "These are my gifts for you." My wife and I were both very shocked and firmly rejected. He didn't listen to us. I grew up in the countryside, so I knew what rice means to a farmer and I didn't think I should take them for free. Jin Dong's brother kept forcing us to receive his presents, and I kept refusing. At that moment, I saw Jin Dong's eyes. His eyes told me how he wished for us to just receive the presents. Suddenly I felt, perhaps, that his way of expressing gratitude was different from mine.

 Maybe he thought merely saying or writing thanks was very superficial. He wanted a more sincere way to express his appreciation.

Suddenly, the Holy Spirit gave me wisdom. I suggested to him, "Why don't I just receive your precious

53

gifts then? I'm really touched. And now, I hope you will receive my present as well." I quickly took out money from my pocket and gave it to him. "This is my present. I hope you can buy warm clothes for your wife and children." He persistently refused it. "If you refuse it, I can't receive your presents, either," I said. He didn't know what to say and finally allowed me to put the money in his pocket.

Jin Dong's brother somehow thought it was not what Jin Dong really wanted. A few days later, he brought 16 packages of rice gave them to us. He said, "This is a real gift; please, just receive them." Seeing the rice, my wife smiled and said, "I complained about our lack of rice and asked God to give us some. And now we have been given a tremendous amount of rice." We happily shared the rice with the dentist, our neighbors and other missionaries as well.

FUNDRAISING FOR THE BLIND

At one point there was a concert in a Japanese church in Beijing to raise money for the blind. Many sponsors from many different organizations participated, including a Japanese record company who gave money and helped with the things that were needed for the event. A Christian Japanese group called "Yuodia" was headlining the event, and a few blind musicians gave recitals. This event was originally planned to commemorate the 36-year amity treaty between China and Japan. There were many obstacles to overcome, including getting an approval from the Secretary of Culture; however, everything eventually went on as planned. This event was extremely special because every one of our members from Jao-Yang Church was able to attend. Previously, every time there was a special event, I felt sad because Chinese nationals were not able to participate (and there were passport checks at the entrances). However, this time, we were able to participate together with our church members and were able to have an event that would be remembered for a long time. I wanted my Chinese brothers and sisters in Christ to realize, even a little bit, how amazing it was to be a believer of Christ. They could contribute to society in a positive way, participating in certain events, influencing those around them and shining the light within their world by applying the gospel to their lives (not just by praying and worshiping in hiding).

After the musical performances ended, I told the 15 Chinese men and women there to apply the things they had felt on that day to their own lives by having a large vision in Christ and acting upon it. We as Christians should act upon what we believe in. Through this event, we were able to gather around 500,000 Yuan ($67,500) and donated it to China's Institution for the Blind. Journalists and reporters from various newspapers and Chinese broadcasting companies covered the event.

OUR NEW CAR: A GIFT FROM HEAVEN

China is one of the fastest developing countries in the world. Due to the preparations for the 2008 Olympics, Beijing seemed to develop and change overnight. The change of pace was getting faster; hence, people's minds and hearts starts to get agitated as they followed the fast moving trends. People don't tend to enjoy and appreciate the little things in life, choosing instead to chase after new and exciting things.

However, life in Beijing was not always great. There were three main things that brought us discomfort. One of them was the climate. Because of the dry weather, there was a lot of dust. Many people suffered from respiratory disorders and people were always longing for fresh air. Secondly, even though people use water purifiers and filters, the water is not clean. People have to buy water, but even that is sometimes fake clean water, so people are always longing for fresh water. Thirdly, Beijing has a very busy and confusing traffic environment with all the bicycles, motorcycles, tricycles and cars on the roads. Foreigners not familiar with the roads often use taxis. However, because of the city expanding and many taxi drivers coming into the city from the countryside, they do not accept passengers when they are asked to take them places with which they are not familiar. Many taxi drivers even take advantage of the passengers and commit serious crimes. A while ago, relatives of my wife's friend came to visit Beijing from Korea. The couple was sitting in a taxi, and suddenly the engine stopped. The driver asked the husband if he could help him push the car from behind. When he got out of the taxi to push the car, the taxi driver started the engine and kidnapped his wife. A few days later, his wife returned with an eye, one of her kidneys, and other organs of her body that used to be a pair missing, now left with one each. These horrific crimes occur quite often.

Of course, horrific crimes occur in many countries around the world, including Korea and America. It is not just a problem in China. However, the more our use of taxis increased, the more stressful it became for me to get into a cab with my wife and three kids. Due to this, every time we went out on a family outing, I was under an extreme amount of pressure and stress. Sometimes taxis would refuse to take us because of the excess number of people, leaving us to wait under the hot sun or in the cold of a winter day. Sometimes we waited for hours for a taxi that would take us to our destination.

Thankfully, knowing our difficult situation, Lexington Presbyterian Church in the States sent us $25,700 for us to buy a van. Also, Nanum Church from Korea sent us $1,000, and we combined the money to buy a 7-seater van suitable for our family's needs. The kids were so excited when we bought the car. I went to pick up my oldest son Segi and found him looking exhausted from a day at school. I rolled down the window of the car and called out to him. He couldn't believe his eyes and just stood there on the sidewalk for a moment or two. Then he screamed, "Wow, Dad! That is a cool car!" That night, Segi volunteered to lead prayer during our family worship. He thanked God for the car He had provided for us. God's provision of a car was such a tremendous encouragement to us and made us truly feel like we were members of the society to which we had come to dedicate our lives.

SPONSORING EVANGELISTS

Ninety percent of the offering that was offered to our church was tithes. We had a policy within our church where we offered sixty percent of the tithes to evangelism and donations. We also decided that we would sponsor evangelists and pastors. We received recommendations from other missionaries and began sponsoring four evangelists. We renewed the contract each year and sent 300 Yuan ($50) every month. One of these evangelists was a man who had visited our church and was able to introduce himself and share how God worked through his life. Many of our church members were challenged and encouraged by the bold faith he had.

THE BIRTH OF THE NEW INTERNATIONAL CHURCH

The New International Church (NIC), a church for returned Chinese émigrés who now have foreign citizenship, was established in October 2007. Other international churches conduct their services only in English, but the NIC does everything in Chinese. Unlike the general international churches that are only for "pure" foreigners, the NIC focuses on Chinese nationals who have taken up foreign citizenship. The establishment of this church was significant in China. It was the first time a church received permission for religious activity under the name of "church" in China. Also, if at least one member in a family possesses foreign citizenship, the whole family can attend the church. The NIC actually has some local Chinese who are part of the leadership in the church. Of course, the church leaders were mostly foreign Chinese except for me.

In the years before the NIC was established, we attended other international churches and made friends with some overseas Chinese. We shared common beliefs about God. We invited them to come over to our house. While having a meal, we shared with each other some suggestions about living in China and beginning a ministry there. Gradually, our relationships became full of trust and kindness. Later on, I found out that they were the people who were ready to lead the NIC. They enthusiastically invited me to join the meeting of pioneering the NIC. Furthermore, I was selected to be part of a team responsible for establishing the NIC. Most missionaries wish to work with local Chinese people, and I was able to. It's truly the grace of God and only He could have done it.

THE DEVELOPMENT OF THE CEO FELLOWSHIP

CEO Fellowship is one of the bigger ministries I was involved in, serving the group as a vice president. It consisted of Christian businessman who are involved in minor enterprises. One year we had a CEO conference in Beijing themed "Responsibility for Society," and nearly 100 businessmen attended. Wonderful speakers came from the United States, Canada and other countries. Such a conference occurring in Beijing was very rare. It challenged every attendee with a new vision. All the attendants were very excited and said, "I couldn't have dreamed about such a wonderful meeting." They were very surprised that there were so many Christian businessmen in Beijing. Also, everyone was pleased that the meeting was public unlike previously, when it had been held secretly. People were discussing how they should manage their property, share the love of God as businessmen and personally live by the words of God.

However, an unwanted situation happened during the conference. Unexpectedly, one of the hotel guards reported the meeting to police. So policemen came and investigated everything over and over again. They soon contacted the highest-ranking officer in Beijing, and he came to investigate. Surprisingly, after he finished looking into the conference program and content, he said, "This conference is being held for a great purpose. It shouldn't be unofficial. Why don't you legalize the conference?" In addition, he told us in detail how we could get legalization for the conference. At that moment, I realized the importance of intercessory prayer. We spent one-and-a-half months writing up our association policy and the proper curriculum and handed it in. As promised, they gave us formal permission to hold the conference and even allowed us to conduct a Bible study during the conference. We came up with a curriculum to train CEOs as well. I would lecture on the subject of "Becoming a Mature Leader" over the course of eight weeks and train small group leaders as well.

We eventually divided the fellowship into two parts, mainly because the corporations differed in size and needs, and also because the differing interests of the CEOs made it difficult to consolidate them into one group. The two new groups were CCF (for CEOs of smaller businesses) and TCCF, Top-Class CEO Fellowship, for CEOs of larger businesses.

The CCF gathered in small groups for Bible studies, and the leaders of each group were trained prior to leading the group. The TCCF would gather and have training sessions together.

We received valuable advice from Dick, an American entrepreneur and chairman of the CEO Fellowship. He said our goal should be to encourage China's Christian CEOs to become salt and light for the entire Chinese society. This would not only expedite the spread of the gospel throughout China, but would also breed honesty and credibility in China's commercial ethics. Just as tiny droplets of water can eventually break a solid rock, we believed that our small faith and obedience would manifest in great works of the Holy Spirit.

Our training program used the following texts as our main training material: the Bible (to give perspective on entrepreneurship, materialism, management, social responsibility and household management), John Maxwell's *Leadership* and *Being a Mature Leader* which I wrote. I was blessed by God be able to train corporate leaders through CCF and TCCF, and serve them as a member of the leadership team. Two of the leaders of CCF and TCCF became precious friends and fellow workers, gifted to me by God.

The first of the two was CT. He was the actual leader for our corporate group. He started believing in Jesus at a church in Taiwan. In the winter of

1992, the Taiwanese church had a week-long revival congregation. During the gathering, a Korean singing group participated and led a big gospel music rally. At that time he had just completed his military service and was a young scientist contemplating on different paths of life. A Christian invited him to the church, but his participation was more about looking for a reason to criticize the church rather than to get God's blessing and to connect with Him. He sat at the back so that he could leave if he wished to. People kept coming in and the women sitting around him were all holding small boxes of tissues. At first he could not understand the purpose of carrying a box of tissues to church and thought that the church played sad hymns to make innocent people cry. A few moments later the sermon began and people started to weep. He felt that the church was for weak people who needed to depend on something spiritual — it was clearly not for him. All of a sudden, a word from the "boring" hymn woke his spirit and the church began to light up. He could see letters amid the light and the letters were spelling out words like "salvation, goodness, love, forgiveness, completeness," words expressing the essence of God.

Paul saw Jesus in the light, and CT saw God's words in the light. He was wrapped with an overwhelming sensation from within and his mind was filled with the thought that he was a sinner and that he had sinned so much in his life. He felt a surge of tears falling from his eyes. He used up two boxes of tissues before he could stop his tears. After this life-changing experience, he graduated from university, worked in a Taiwanese science lab (an institute equivalent to America's Institute of Science and Technology), flew to the United States to complete his masters in Berkeley University, and was finally called to go to China by God. He was currently in charge of a small company in Beijing and serving in the CCF group. He also married a Chinese woman. He was my best friend, a student to whom I taught the Bible and a very humble person. I once asked him about his dream and he said that it was to become more humble.

The second of the two was SH. Ever since he was young, he had led a poor and unfortunate life because his father was an intellectual and the entire family was branded enemies of the state. One day, people from the movie industry came to his elementary school looking for child actors to star in a new movie, and SH was chosen. For the first time in his life, he was starring in a movie with beautiful actresses. Numerous successful movies followed and soon he became the part of the next generation of high society. He continued to star in 19 more movies and became a famous actor. In the early 1980s, the government lifted the iron curtain in China and SH was among the first generation of Chinese to live overseas. When he arrived in New Zealand, he realized how poor he was. At that time, no matter how much Chinese Yuan he had, it could only just cover school tuition in U.S. dollars, and he was forced to work all sorts of odd jobs. He started attending a nearby church in New Zealand and came to believe in Jesus. A few years later, his new business in Australia became a big success, and he received the right of permanent residence and was able to return to Beijing, where the rest of his family was, as a successful businessman.

Nineteen years ago, China was a country closed to outside influence, so there were officially only two churches in Beijing. During this time, Billy Graham secretly entered China. SH translated Billy Graham's sermons, and the people who were listening covered their faces with their coats so that they could not be identified. After the sermon, SH would give a late-night tour of Beijing to Billy Graham in his car; at that time, cars were scarce. SH and Billy Graham went to Tienanmen Square and stood on the spot where Mao Zedong declared China a socialist country and they proclaimed that a million Chinese people would one day gather there to say, "Hallelujah." Then out of the darkness the police came to capture them. They ran for about 20 minutes through Beijing's alleyways back to where the car was parked. When SH dropped Graham off at his hotel and returned to his apartment, four policemen were waiting for him. After a long interrogation, he was given three options: to be deported and never return, to be imprisoned for seven years or to live a secluded life in the highlands. For the first time he discussed his situation with his fiancée Sarah. SH's father, who was at the time a lawyer and a college professor, had introduced his student, Sarah, to SH. SH did not love her nor acknowledge her as his wife, but he felt that he should discuss the situation with her, so they had a deep and honest conversation. Sarah told him that being deported would be a bad idea since he would not be able to return. She suggested he go back to the police station and confess and admit to what had happened. She also promised that, should he be imprisoned, she would move near the prison to provide food and take care of him no matter how long it took for him to be released.

That night he was imprisoned and had to confess everything he had done. The police knew all about him, even the fact that he was interpreting for Billy Graham. Then one of the policemen in the interrogation room said that when he was young his family was so poor they starved almost every day and that there had been a Christian neighbor who brought them bread every now and then. He told the other policemen that SH had not committed theft nor had he preached to others and that he was simply interpreting, since there was no one else who could speak English. He also suggested that they should let SH off since he was a well-known Chinese actor and the situation could get complicated. The other policeman agreed, and after getting his signature on the necessary documents, SH was allowed to go home. They even offered him a ride home in the police car.

SH was the host for one of the CEO conferences, and with his wit and sense of humor, he successfully led the conference.

THE TEARS OF A CHINESE SISTER

One day, a Chinese sister who heard the gospel from us came to my house and told us delightful stories. That year, she had graduated with a major in Chinese and already had a job. She was chosen from among thirty students to become a teacher in the international department at Beijing Foreign Language University. She cried as she told me the story, and I had never seen her in such an emotional state. That university was the one she desperately wanted to go to, and now she would be teaching there. She knew the other students who had competed with her were very capable, so she did not expect to get the position. She said, "This is such a blessing, by the grace of God." That was the first time I had heard her use such an expression. She kept saying, "I really don't know how I got in. There were plenty of brilliant people. How was it they couldn't get in, but I did?"

I also couldn't understand some parts of her story. I asked her if when she filled out the application form whether there was a place to put her religion. She said, "Of course there was. I wrote 'Christian'." There were many foreign students learning Chinese at the university, especially the international department. Surely there must be some Christians in the department, I thought.

Many young people, after becoming Christians, are unwilling to join the Communist Party for theological reasons and the conscience of their faith. Therefore, many of them are not willing to become Christians, thinking that Christianity will be a barrier to their future. Some people had even heard the gospel and wanted to be Christians, but actually postponed receiving Jesus. However, this Chinese sister was different. She officially revealed that she was a Christian. It really impressed me. God was glorified by a word she wrote, 'Christian,' on the application form.

CHINESE STUDENT MISSIONS IN TOKYO

Japan is a country that has a special meaning for me. I spent part of my life in Japan studying. It was there that I heard the gospel, was spiritually born again and was baptized. I helped a missionary plant a church in Japan, and it was there that I was called by God to be His servant.

I started to feel a burden for evangelizing Chinese students in Japan. I was always looking for an opportunity to meet with church leaders in Japan to discuss this with them. One day, a Chinese couple (K and Esther) from our church was dispatched to Japan by their company. I felt my very ambiguous plan might become a reality. Also, our mission agency had encouraged me to take a holiday in Japan, so I took that as a sign from God. Fortunately, my mother-in-law was coming to Beijing and could help look after our children.

Before heading to Japan, I sent an e-mail to the people I was going to meet there and told them my schedule. When I arrived in Narita Airport, I found out the people picking me up were neither Korean nor Japanese. They were the Chinese couple, Esther and K.

In going to Japan, I felt many different emotions. It reminded me of the spring I spent there and the passion I had. I went to the church that I had established with another missionary 17 years before. However, the church had divided into three different churches due to disunity. I was both disappointed and shocked. I had actually heard the story before, but personally seeing the condition of the churches and hearing the reason for the separation shocked me. Nevertheless, I took it as God's providence and decided to visit all three churches.

One of the churches was a Japanese congregation of 30 under the care of a devoted Korean missionary named Lee Young Sook. The second church, named Tokyo Logos Life Church, was made up of nearly 120 Korean students. These students looked just like me 17 years ago, fervently keeping the faith. What surprised me most were the 10 Japanese and 6-7 Chinese people also at the church. I was so pleased and encouraged Esther and K to attend this church so that someday they might be able to plant a Chinese church. They seemed to be having the same thoughts as I was and happily agreed with me. The pastor was especially open-minded about missions in China. We met together and enthusiastically discussed the prospect of planting a Chinese church.

The third church, Tokyo Seisyo Church, was where I got baptized and was like my mother church. It was there that I again met two people whom I respected, senior pastor Oyama and elder Hirosaki. We spent two hours talking about the past. We shared our ideas on the necessity of Chinese missions and I asked them to consider planting a Chinese church in the same way that the Korean church had been planted 17 years before. They said they would try their best to provide a Chinese service in the church.

Through this opportunity, my long desire for Japan was appeased. I praised the Lord for showing me the prospect of a good future for Chinese students in Japan.

APPLES OF GOLD

A wonderful Bible study we know is called *Apples of Gold*. We were finally able to use it in China. My wife and I prayed about it and spent three months preparing a place, helpers, teachers and meeting other needs. We started with eight Chinese members and from the first day, it was amazing.

Apples of Gold is a nurturing program for women. Its lessons focus on the family and its target audience is young stay-at-home moms, especially mothers of preschoolers. The issues covered included kindness, loving your children, loving your husband, submission, purity and hospitality. The program would take six weeks and each week, a different mentor would deliver a lecture. My wife learned of this Bible study from Annette Murray and the wives of other professors at Columbia International University.

During the first hour, the young women would learn to cook a meal. During the following 50 minutes, they would eat the dishes they had just cooked while studying the Bible and having table discussions. Thus, attendees would receive both physical and spiritual food. Food is an important part of Chinese culture, and so, coupling a cooking class with Bible study is not only an extremely effective way of reaching Chinese women, but also an efficient use of their time.

The number of families with parents who are separated is dramatically increasing in China. A recent report showed that over 60% of married couples over the age of 20 are getting a divorce. Through this Bible study, these young women learned how to build and have a stable family.

Note: You will find more information about Apples of Gold and reports from several of the women who went through the program in Appendix A. These reports will give you insight into how to meet women's physical and spiritual needs.

PLANTING THE SECOND CHURCH

We had been trying to plant a second church for a year, but there was no suitable location so it kept getting delayed. We finally had a service in the office of H, one of our training leaders. We invited 12 people to the first service, but only seven came. That morning I preached at our Jao-Yang Church and was headed to Wang Jing, our new home church, but there were traffic jams and I was 35 minutes late. Fortunately, when I arrived at Wang Jing, others had been delayed as well. The sermon I was going to preach was about reputation or "losing face." There were also two newcomers, sisters, so I preached the gospel to them. One of the sisters, Lu, who was a Chinese-English interpreter at her company, accepted Jesus as her Savior after listening to the gospel in detail. The other sister, Wu, who was working in a Hong Kong company, observed closely how her sister Lu received Jesus, and she soon received Jesus as well.

In China, if anyone expressed objection after hearing the gospel, the rest of the group would get confused and eventually fail to accept Jesus. After experiencing this several times, I developed a strategy to share the gospel one-on-one, and to pray for them to accept the Lord one-by-one.

After the service, as usual, we had a meal. I asked Wu, who had just received Jesus, whether she had a boyfriend. I don't usually ask that kind of question, but for some reason, I did. As soon as I asked her, she very quietly began to talk about her boyfriend. He had recently been in an accident at his company that had left his whole body paralyzed. One of the other workers at the company had been using a big machine and during a stressful situation, he turned the machine to the wrong side. Just then Wu's boyfriend was passing by, and the machine hit him on the back of his head. He suffered a serious wound. Wu told me that her boyfriend could have avoided the injury if he had been standing only 10 centimeters ahead or behind, or if he had been passing by there one second earlier or later. Her boyfriend had three surgeries on his head, neck and waist, but he was still totally paralyzed from the waist down. The doctor said he would be permanently disabled. Wu just hoped that one day her boyfriend would be able to walk. I stopped eating and asked all the members to pray for her boyfriend. After we prayed, I told her, "If your boyfriend is able to walk, you have to believe that it was healing from God, and that he worked through our prayer. She said, "If it really happens, I will."

Two days later, our church leader, H, gave me a call. She said, "Wu's boyfriend suddenly stood up from his wheelchair and walked down the stairs from the third floor to the first floor!" In addition, H said the Holy Spirit wanted her to go and share the gospel with him. I said that was a great idea. The next day at a leadership training meeting, I asked whether Wu's boyfriend had received Jesus. H said that she hadn't gone to see him yet — she had only prayed. I said, "How come you didn't quickly obey the words of the Holy Spirit?" She answered, "Oh! Is that right? I thought we were all going to go and share the gospel with him."

You see, in the older generation in China, they are accustomed to the division of labor practiced in the Communist Party, so they are very reluctant to work if they do not have definitive instruction. Many foreign businessmen confront difficulties with this. When a foreigner instructs the Chinese to do a task, they only do the work they know how to specifically perform. Most Chinese don't know how to handle all of the work and are afraid they will make a mistake, so it is necessary to divide the work up among them and explain the instructions clearly so that everything will go smoothly. That day, I understood better why it was important to give specific instructions. After the meeting, I told H that she should go directly to see Wu's boyfriend and share the gospel with him.

We also prayed together for this work. I knew that it would take nearly two hours to get the hospital, so I said to her, "In the bus, pray again. Think about the way you are going to evangelize to him. Think about the method you learned in class." Four hours later, I received a long phone message. It said, "Wu's boyfriend received Jesus. He has started to read the Bible now. Moreover, his parents showed interest in the gospel message as well. So tomorrow I am going to go to the hospital again, this time to share the gospel with his parents." The next day, his parents accepted Jesus as their Savior through H's faithful work. Wu's sister also received Jesus, and not more than a week later she evangelized to another person and brought him to church the next Sunday.

We sometimes get our most precious instruction from the Lord in difficulty. Wu's boyfriend met Jesus during the hardest time of his life, and because of it, his whole family also received Jesus.

A MIRACLE IN A HOSPITAL WARD

From then on, whenever I prayed, I couldn't help thinking about Wu's boyfriend M, so I asked H, the leader of Wang Jing Church, to visit him and pray for him, his family and the other patients in his room. When H got there, all the people in the room welcomed her with bright smiles. H was able to sense that there was a big change in the room after M's conversion to Christ. M could not previously walk, but he was healed, and this gave hope to the other patients. There, H shared the gospel, and right away four patients and another four people—the patients' caretakers—accepted Jesus. One brother from Hanam confessed, "All my family members are Christians except me, but now I am really glad that I became a Christian as well. If Jesus heals me and lets me walk again, I will offer the compensation money that I received for the accident to a church, and live the rest of my life for Jesus as an evangelist." And two weeks later when H visited the hospital again, the man was not there; he had been completely healed and had walked home. According to H, the doctor in charge of that room of patients said that only God could perform this kind of miracle. It was no wonder that the doctor said that, because that hospital room was specifically for patients being kept alive in barely vegetative states.

LOVE FOR AN ENEMY

Yan was a woman who used to work for a British bank in England and was currently a CEO of an Internet-related company. She became a member of our church despite my poor preaching in Chinese. Her spiritual growth was so rapid that I had her join my leadership training course. One day, she told me about her marital crisis. Her husband, who was an American, wanted a divorce. We prayed for her family, but the situation grew even worse. Her husband brought his new girlfriend Z into the house, and Yan had to give up her bedroom to Z.

One Sunday, I recognized a female newcomer sitting near Yan. I asked Yan about the new face and found out that she was Z. She came to believe Jesus through Yan's evangelism. I wanted to give Z a few verses from the Scripture but I couldn't think of any, so I decided to talk with her after the service. I asked Z, "Do you know what kind of sin you have committed?"

To my surprise, she earnestly acknowledged her sin. I said to her that she had to repent and leave the house right away. She said, "Now that I believe in Jesus, I will do what the Bible tells me to do." Having seen what happened, Yan thanked me several times. On my way home, the following verses came to my mind: "But I tell you who hear me: Love your enemies, do good to those who hate you, bless those who curse you, pray for those who mistreat you" (Luke 6:27-28) and "Blessed are the poor in spirit, for theirs is the kingdom of heaven" (Matthew 5:3).

A couple of days later I heard from Yan that Z had left with all of her belongings. Yan's Communist parents had been angry at God. If God exists, they said, how could God treat their daughter Yan like this. However, through all the pain, they also accepted Jesus as their Savior.

H'S CHANGE OF HEART

H was a leader at Wang Jing Church. When we first met her, she was struggling with depression after her husband's death. Her Christian faith was mixed with Shamanism and other beliefs, and it seemed that she had not received proper training in Christianity. We gave her three suggestions: first, she must not depend on people, but only trust God. I made it clear to her that what prevented her from being blessed by God was merely herself. Secondly, we told her that it is impossible to serve two masters, that is, money and God. She should first seek the kingdom of God (Matthew 6:33). Our third suggestion was to simplify her spiritual life. Because she thought everything spiritual was good, she accepted all kinds of things that seemed to be spiritual. She embraced our advice and obeyed us. In only a few months, she was transformed into a spiritually healthy person. I was convinced by her inner change and appointed her as a leader of Wang Jing Church.

One day, H called me and asked me to tell her family members (her parents, older sister and two nieces) about Jesus. She said that it was beyond her ability to change her family. Hearing that, I felt burdened, because I knew that salvation comes from God, not from man. After my wife and I fasted and prayed for her family, we invited them to our house. One of our strategies of evangelism was to utilize our family as a team. That is, people who came to our house have become open-minded through the good meals served by my wife and the entertainment presented by my children. That day, our family did our best and three among the five guests seemed to have hearts softened toward the gospel. However, the two who were negative forced the other three not to give their hearts to the Lord. As a result, all the guests returned home without having made a decision. My heart was disappointed.

The very next day, H sent me a text message saying that her parents would like to come again to me so I could pray for them. I told her that she could pray for them herself and that we also would pray for them to invite Jesus into their hearts. I wanted her to know that the Holy Spirit in me dwelt in her as well. After a couple of hours, I heard from her that her parents accepted Jesus as their Savior. What was more amazing was that her mother's cancer lump disappeared, for which all her family members praised God.

In order to establish the early church, God allowed many miracles. God continues to perform the same miracles in China to build up His church.

THE FIRST LEADERSHIP TRAINING COURSE

The four leaders in the leadership training course tasted heaven on a daily basis. Through a three-week-long training they became powerful evangelists who usually brought 10 to 20 people to the church each month. We planned to have a three-hour session for each training session, but it usually took us longer to share our testimonies with one another. I was confident that they were some of the best evangelists in China. They were also confident in themselves because they had learned how to be submissive to the guidance of the Holy Spirit. In addition to showing the variety of evangelism methods, I emphasized that they should be sensitive to the way the Holy Spirit works—He works in various ways for different people in different situations. I also stressed to them that they should give up all their own ways and be obedient to the Spirit, which would consequently free them from the burden of artificial evangelism. Then they could enjoy and vitalize evangelism in the power of the Spirit, and evangelism could become their joy and pleasure.

"I BELIEVE THAT GOD IS ALIVE"

A senior student, M, began to attend our church along with his friend. From the first visit, he appeared to come in order to investigate something rather than to believe in Jesus. He seemed to be curious about Christianity. Four weeks later, I approached M and shared the gospel. As soon as I asked him if he would like to accept Jesus, to all our surprise, he got upset and started yelling at me. Up to that point he had been quietly listening and following what I was explaining to him. I was confused by his unexpected reaction. He resisted emphatically by saying, "God is love, and I don't need Jesus as a mediator to have fellowship with God; this is my belief and faith!"

I sensed that an evil spirit was working in him because on the same day another student who had come along with M also got angry and vehemently rejected to the gospel. Unfortunately, it was time to leave for Wang Jing Church , so I left those two students in the care of one of the church leaders. On my way out, I spoke to M, "Think about the possibility that your conviction could be wrong. We can talk more later." On my way to Wang Jing Church, I felt guilty because it was like I had shuffled my responsibility onto others. Later, I heard that the leader couldn't do anything but give them a booklet titled "Evidences of the Gospel."

After M and his friend returned to their dormitory, they read the booklet and had a discussion. In the middle of their discussion, something strange happened to both of them. First, they heard some strange sounds from their ears and felt something on their backs traveling from their waists toward their necks. Then suddenly it was pulled out of their necks. At the same time, both of them started to speak tongues that they could not understand. They were bewildered because they did not know what was taking place. Then, M told his friend that he was going to believe in Jesus, but his friend left the room in a hurry saying that he was too terrified to decide anything.

Later that day, M found a wallet in the hallway. When he opened it up to see how much was in it, he found five 10-won bills and three 1-won bills, which made a total of 53 won. He showed the wallet to other students to find out who had lost it. The students gathered around him and asked him how much was in it. M said it had 53 won. However, when M opened the wallet again to confirm the amount, there was only one 100-won bill. M could not believe his eyes. Looking at the 100-won bill, M's friends told him off for telling a lie.

M was perplexed and didn't know what to do about it. One of the students suggested calling the owner of the wallet to check the amount. They located a student ID card in the wallet and obtained his number. When they called and asked how much was in the wallet, he said there might be five 10-won bills and a couple of 1-won bills. But there they were, still looking at the 100-won bill. About 30 minutes later, the owner arrived at the dormitory, and he opened up his wallet. This time, all of them standing there could not find the 100-won bill, but five 10-won bills and three 1-won bills as M had originally insisted.

That incident became big news in the dormitory. Finally, M reached the conclusion that God had performed a miracle for his sake because he kept doubting and was rebellious against God. At that point, he could not hold it inside him anymore, so he called one of the leaders at the church to ask for help. M begged the leader to help him to accept Jesus. Then, on the following Sunday, in front of the whole congregation, M confessed, "I believe that God is alive and I also believe in Jesus as my Savior." He reminded me of Paul, who once was a persecutor of Jesus and His followers, but later became an apostle of Christ after having met Jesus on his way to Damascus.

When M shared his testimony, all the church members were envious of M for the unique experience. Some people even looked discouraged that they had never experienced such a thing. So I read John 20:25-29 about Thomas: "Then Jesus told him, 'Because you have seen me, you have believed; blessed are those who have not seen and yet have believed.'" I explained what the passage meant. When I saw them smiling again, I was relieved. I told them that some people come to God through miracles, but they should be very cautious against biased mysticism which only seeks miraculous signs. I emphasized that the most wonderful miracle would be to believe in the Bible as the unchangeable Word of God and to live faithfully by it.

OUR THIRD CHRISTMAS IN CHINA

Most of the churches in Beijing celebrated Christmas in a suburban area for safety reasons, which made me feel uncomfortable. I thought we should be bold enough to have a Christmas party inside the city where we served the people. Amazingly, God had prepared a beautiful place for us to celebrate Jesus' birthday. CN, one of the leaders in Jao-Yang Church, was an interior designer and had recently worked for a large Chinese restaurant that was scheduled to open on December 24. By God's grace, the owner of the restaurant granted us use of the place for a Christmas party even before the opening. The restaurant was located in the center of Beijing; we were able to have a great Christmas service inside the city as we had prayed! I am sure that the restaurant was blessed because it was used for such a precious purpose.

Before the Christmas service, we gathered in a closed room with only a few people. In there, six Chinese brothers and sisters were baptized by a pastor from Japan. I assume that it is quite natural for spiritual workers to want to baptize people that they taught and ministered to, but in China it is illegal to baptize, so they had to invite pastors from other areas to come over and baptize new believers.

Looking at the six people rejoicing at the baptism, I was able to see what the baptism of the Spirit is like. All of them were full of the Spirit and served others with love and loyalty throughout the Christmas party. I felt that the love and unity of the early church described in Acts had been revealed again in this land. Their love and transforming attitudes taught me to grow in my faith. It is not I, but rather they, who teach what true faith is like by living a pure, faithful, and obedient life.

After the baptism, everyone assembled in an open area. Even though I decided not to care about the numbers of people attending the service, inwardly I was expecting a large number of people so as to show off to the Korean intercessory prayer team I had invited. What a poor man I was!

On that day a total of 70 people showed up, and 12 out of 20 newcomers accepted Jesus. When the man who led the service said, "Stand up if you would like to invite Jesus into your heart," I thought to myself that it was an awkward calling. As far as I knew, the Chinese culture was concerned about saving face, so people were quite reluctant to come forward and take charge of their action before others. I thought that he should have asked people to close their eyes and raise their hands silently if they would like to believe in Jesus. But after a few more invitations, people started to stand up. Then, he said to those who were standing to come up to the stage, which I thought was nonsense. I said to myself that he had gone too far and that such a demand was too much for the people. However, much to my surprise, those who were standing made their way to the stage through the crowd. It was not until they were standing on the stage that I realized how seriously they took the altar call. Twelve lost sheep were returned to the Lord that night.

In fact, the Christmas party had not been prepared by me, but by some of our Chinese brothers. I placed the responsibilities on them for two reasons: first, if I were to plan it, it would be a Korean or American-style Christmas event, and second, I wanted to see how the Chinese understood Christmas in terms of their culture. It turned out to be a remarkable performance considering the short period of time they had for preparation. The drama portion was especially amazing. They memorized all their lines and played their roles like real actors and actresses. Some of the workers in the restaurant were touched by the drama and opened their hearts to the gospel. Due to security reasons, we could not share the good news with them at that time, but we planned to get in touch with them later. The sister of the restaurant's owner had already given her heart to the Lord when one of the leaders of the church spoke with her about renting the place for our Christmas party. The manager of the restaurant also appeared to be interested in Christianity through the service. As we were cleaning the place, my wife said to the family of the owner, "If your employees want to believe in Jesus, please encourage them to do so. If they believe in Jesus, they will work harder and serve customers with integrity because they will know that God will look after them."

The following day, I heard from the leader of Jao-Yang Church about the conversion of a Muslim woman. In fact, she had been the first to come up to the stage the night before. It is hard for any missionary to bring a Muslim to the Lord in his or her lifetime, so this was a real blessing. He added that a group of Chinese policemen had came in to eat right after we had finished the closing prayer, but they did not notice what kind of event we had held at the restaurant. Trouble was averted due to the intercessory prayers of the saints, and God protected us from all harm.

Jao-Yang Church again participated in sending Christmas presents to an orphanage. Wang Jing Church also had planned to send gifts to the poor people. Since it was the second time we were sending presents to the cleaning company employees, all the preparations went much more quickly. My wife called the company and found that there were 70 workers in total (10 more people than the year before), and our church family set to wrapping gifts.

Four women from Wang Jing Church, including my wife, went to the company with the gifts we had prepared. H, a leader of Wang Jing Church, asked me what to say to them, and I said, "Just tell them that you have come to share the love of Jesus with small Christmas gifts, and then do as the Holy Spirit leads." It was fun to see the four women heading off with big bundles in both hands. They looked like soldiers on a special mission. The company was located nearby, so I thought they should be back within ten minute or so. Thirty minutes passed, but they did not come back. I began to worry because at Christmas time the police often raided the streets, and it was already dark outside. At last, the four female "soldiers" came back, very excited. As soon as they sat around the table, they prayed a short prayer and began to cry, then reported what had happened.

When they arrived at the gate, two of the workers were waiting for them. As they went into the office, the female boss of the company welcomed my wife, saying that she remembered her. When we visited them last year, there were only 14 people in the office; the others had already gone home. This year, the boss held my wife's hands and thanked her for the visit. My wife also thanked the boss for the opportunity for us to share the love of God and asked her if she wanted to believe in Jesus. Unexpectedly, she said yes. My wife asked the people standing there the same question, and most of them said yes. She went on to ask them to raise their hands if they really meant it, and this time all of them put their hands up. She wanted to make sure of their decision, so told them to come toward her. Again, all of them moved toward her including the boss.

At that moment, the Holy Spirit touched my wife, and she delivered a short message: "I myself went to a foreign country to make money. It was really hard to be away from my family, and I spent many days in tears. During the hardest time of my life, I met Jesus, and He comforted me and gave me heavenly peace. Since then, I no longer cried out over my destiny. Even though what you are doing for a living is difficult, I hope you will be able to experience the true peace and joy that Jesus gives. We can gain wisdom no matter what work we do, and when we are grateful for everything, there will be more things to be thankful for. I will ask you one more time. Do you really want to believe in Jesus, or are you just following your boss? In believing in Jesus, there are two very important things: love and forgiveness. God loved us so much that He gave His one and only Son in order to save us from sin and death. Everyone who believes in Jesus will be forgiven. And you also have to forgive those who have done wrong to you."

Since all of them said they wanted to accept Jesus voluntarily, my wife had H lead prayer for them. Many of them were crying. My wife added: "Now that Jesus lives in you, work hard to get to know Him better by reading the Bible, and have fellowship with Him through prayer. When you pray, He hears." Then, she taught them how to pray and made sure that they ended their prayers by saying 'in Jesus' name.'

A week later, H called the boss to find out how many Bibles they needed. After checking with the workers, she asked for 30 Bibles, so we sent 31 to them. Some time later, I heard from one of the workers that they were reading their Bibles on their beds every night.

That same Christmas we received packages from the States and from South Korea. The packages reflected the givers in that the people in the States asked us what we needed and sent us the items we wanted, while the items from Korea were prepared according to their leading by the Spirit during prayer. Either way, all the gifts we received were exactly what we needed.

Each time the parcels arrived, we all had fun opening them. While opening the box from the States, we could detect an American scent. As we unpacked the popcorn and coffee, the children shouted for joy. The jackets for the children fit well. Looking at the presents, I could sense that God was encouraging us in our sweat and toil for the lost in China. Indeed, God rewarded us for our work this way.

Some of our Chinese brethren shared words with us to send to the congregations abroad who were supporting us. Here's what they had to say:

"I thank God for sending you guys here to us and letting me get to know you. Thank you for the love you have shown to us and for your teaching of the Word. I also thank God that I could see what a Christian couple and family are like." – Lee

"Praise the Lord for sending the best Bible teacher to us. I thank God that He has chosen you and me to become members of His family." - Yan

"God may be very pleased with your being in China. This is what God told me to let you know." – Tan

"It has been a blessing to us that your family came to China. Thank you, God!" – Chen

"Before I met you, I was a prodigal son. Through your ministry, I have come near to God. I love you." – Deng

"In 2007, I have too many things to be thankful for. Most of all, I'm grateful that I am serving INC with you. May the grace and blessings of God be with your family forever." – CK

TRAINING MORE LEADERS

After concentrating on leadership training for a year and a half, everyone had reached the level capable of leading a small group for themselves. Each leader would report effective teaching methods and strategies learned as well as any problems experienced. This enabled the leaders to accelerate their development, and both the leader and the followers mutually learned from each another. Because China is a large country, each region needed to be approached using different methods so the sharing of know-how and experience was extremely important.

The small group leaders were required to report every week and answer four questions:

1. What did I do and how was it done?
2. What were the participants like?
3. What problems were identified?
4. What lessons were learned?

These reports helped the leaders to assess themselves, develop capabilities to analyze, ascertain the direction for further development, enhance their problem-solving abilities and ultimately, to understand how they should appropriately lead their followers. We followed Paul's strategy not to build upon another's foundation (Romans 15:20). The leaders were to introduce Christianity to five to seven people, and then they needed to care for them and lead prayer sessions, including a group Bible study. Almost all the small groups had new members joining every week wanting to praise God, so the groups grew very quickly. Every leader had the fundamental ability to introduce Christianity to people, care for new members, and develop and train new followers.

One example was CQ Church. While delivering supplies to people who lost their homes during the Sichuan earthquake, I was traveling in a car with a Christian professor, J, who came from CQ city. During the 3-hour ride I told him about the most effective ways to introduce the gospel to the Chinese based on the methods I had developed.

Sometime after this conversation, he officially requested professional training, and I accepted his request as I saw the passion inside him for lost souls. I asked him to come to Beijing to attend the development training session, and his wife came along. For the first four days I personally trained him and on the fifth day a Chinese trainee of our team led the session. My wife also shared about the importance of family, serving guests and marriage. After a week of training the couple, we sent them back to CQ. Two days after arriving in CQ, they sent us their first report. The report included news that after believing in God, he, for the first time, delivered the gospel to non-believers and introduced them to Christianity. In addition, he wanted to know how he should continue. I told him to do exactly what he was taught in Beijing and to start leading small prayer sessions.

The professor and his wife started small prayer sessions and Bible study groups at the house of a Christian friend. In one month, the couple shared the gospel with 16 people and the group expanded to a total of 18 members. For those who could not attend the Sunday session, the couple would wholeheartedly provide personal training during the week. This was a true sacrifice. When I looked at them, I could feel that God was alive and spreading His Word.

THE SICHUAN EARTHQUAKE

On May 12, 2008, a great earthquake hit Sichuan Province in Western China. The impact was so great that Beijing, a two-and-a-half-hour plane ride away, experienced a 3.0 magnitude earthquake. Although media broadcasted that it was an 8.0 magnitude earthquake, looking at the horrible sight of destroyed buildings and mountains, people argued that it must have been at least an 8.5 magnitude earthquake. People at church were disconcerted, and I said to members, "We do not know why such a disaster occurred, but we do know what we should do from now on. We need to collect as much aid as quickly as possible and help the victims." The congregation was united as one and gave monetary offerings as well as material goods. Our home churches prepared a variety of medical aids, 50 tents and monetary offerings. Church leaders at the international church worked as a team by reaching out to those at the site of the earthquake with about 500 tents. (At that time, I served the international church as the Director of Missions , and also served three home churches I planted.)

In fact, it was my second time visiting Sichuan. My first visit to Sichuan had been exactly 12 days before the great earthquake occurred. Our family had gone to a panda park, which was near the site of the earthquake, in order to attend a missionary meeting. On our way back home, we stopped by a very beautiful valley. Now, the beautiful valley no longer existed. The only evidence we had of its prior existence were several pictures we had taken of it. I remember seeing many insects coming up to the ground as though they were communicating with one another about the natural disaster that was going to happen soon. Had the earthquake occurred 12 days earlier, our family could not have avoided the same disaster.

When I arrived at the earthquake site with an NGO team from the international church, the sight before us was appalling. It looked as if artillery fire had swept away the city in a war. It was an absolutely deserted land. Around 800 houses out of 1200 in one village were completely destroyed. Cities near the place of origin of the earthquake looked like a huge heap of trash. Nonetheless, ambulances and aid carriers from many different churches were busy moving back and forth. At the terrible sight of disaster, I prayed to God asking what to do. I was able to remain clear-headed amid the calamity thanks to my past experiences of earthquakes while I was studying in Japan and the incessant effort of the Japanese government to educate its people in case of emergency.

When an earthquake occurs, the needs vary within a very sensitive time frame. For instance, the needs that must be met within three days and after three days of the occurrence are different. That is why I wanted to go to the earthquake site as quickly as possible. Yet, only a few people were willing to go with me because 6.0-magnitude aftershocks continued to occur. When I asked those who had once loudly said that we must hurry to help the victims, they all refused to go with me, making up all kinds of excuses. Usually airplanes going to Cheng Du, a city with 10 million people, in the Sichuan Province are full; however, due to the earthquake, the airplane was as empty as if we had rented it out for ourselves.

I asked around to friends and churches that supported us to pray for the earthquake in Sichuan. Our safety was not guaranteed then because the aftershocks were still severe. Moreover, as a husband and a father of three children, I needed my family's consent and understanding. Later I found out that my oldest son, who was then eight years old, prayed when I left for the earthquake site, saying: "Dear God, please look out for my daddy so that he can come back home alive and safely."

We arrived at the earthquake site exactly a week after the earthquake. On the first day of our arrival, we drove around to survey the site, and the next day we went to the area where the earthquake had hit the hardest.

Scenic valley before earthquake..

This area would be buried by landslides.

Panda park we visited before earthquake.

Empty flight, normally packed.

Earthquake damage.

Buildings reduced to rubble.

It took us over two hours just to get there from Cheng Du. In the car, I happened to sit next to a professor from the Chong Ching University and taught him how to share the Gospel. He thanked me for the lesson, and was pleased to have met someone who explained to him the true meaning of the Gospel for the first time after he became a Christian. He told me that he gained enough confidence to spread the Gospel, something he hadn't known how to do, thus leaving him unable to evangelize people. Later, this brother in Christ really became an evangelist; since then, together with his wife, he has led over 100 people to God in two years.

After two hours of driving, we finally got to the refugee camp, located in a city closest to the earthquake's epicenter. Over 10,000 people were living in tents on the side of dusty roads. Some people were sleeping and others talking on the phone. Some were just sitting still, looking at the people and cars passing by. The day was hot, and they were enveloped by a cloud of dust whenever cars passed by on the road.

One of our team members approached a policeman and asked him how we could help the victims. He kindly took us to the city government office building. We met with the chief director of the disaster relief center of the city government and inquired what plans the city government had made for the victims. He answered that he did not know what to do because of the massive influx of victims into the area at one time. We told him that we had brought some aid and tents for the victims, and asked if he could have the city government provide us with an appropriate size plot of land for building tents, evenly distribute the aid among the victims, and continue to manage the tent site. I added that we would let the church and the governmental department of religion in Beijing know about the active cooperation of the city government. The chief director assured us in a very kind and engaging manner that he would help us. The city government wrote our church a registration receipt for the tents and aid materials we had brought. They also signed a simple cooperation agreement. Chinese people normally refuse to sign documents that ask for consent in fear of interrogation in the future. As promised, the city government provided a large piece of land for building tents, and also mobilized soldiers to speed up the moving in process for the victims. Angela, our sister in Christ, stayed on after our departure in order to overlook the victims' camp project.

We returned to Cheng Du and stayed overnight at an inexpensive hotel. Many people, in fear of the probability of another earthquake, slept on the side of road, in a playground at a school or on the ground in a park. I was so exhausted that I crashed into bed in the hotel room.

The next day, we took medical supplies, 50 tents, and monetary offerings sent from Jao Yang church to the local church whose building had collapsed due to the earthquake. We asked them to use the monetary offering for reconstruction of the Sunday school at church. Pastor, elders, and deacons of this church expressed their gratitude.

MY THIRD VISIT TO SICHUAN

My third visit to Sichuan along with an NGO team was a month after the earthquake. Chapin Church, our supporting church, sent us $3,000 in aid for the victims. We offered the money to the international church, and the offering, together with other offerings, was spent on the purchase of 105,000 water bottles. Upon receiving the gift, the senior pastor of the international church sent a thank you email to Chapin Church right away. One needs to be careful and must have wisdom and transparency when it comes to using the church's supplies so that he or she will not be tempted by Satan to do evil.

The summer of Sichuan was at its peak. Although the earthquakes had eased, the heaps of collapsed building remnants still remained here and there. This time, the International Church's NGO teams brought 500 tents (larger than the first 500 tents), 105,000 (1.6 liter) water bottles, and 130 bicycles to the people who were stuck in the mountain.

I wanted to bring the Bible with me to restore the victims' spirituality. I distributed five Bibles to each member to bring; however, there were only a few Bibles due to a small number of people who were willing to come. I sent a box of Bibles via airplane. I put a sticker that said 'Victim goods' on the box full of Bibles. At the time, this action took much courage, and God truly protected me.

There were three purposes of our visit:

1. To check if the 105,000 bottles of water arrived and were appropriately delivered to the victims.
2. To deliver aid to places where the need was great.
3. To negotiate with the Department of Health of the city in order to provide continuous aid to the people and families who were affected and disabled by the earthquake.

A bad day to take the bus.

Collapsed floors in a school.

Survivors living on the roadside.

A shipment of tents we purchased.

Relief supplies—500 tents, 130 bicycles.

Unloading relief supplies.

Demonstrating tent set-up.

A completed tent.

Military personnel setting up tent village.

Tent village for earthquake survivors.

Unloading water shipment.

Company where we shared the Gospel.

Disabled people were not receiving proper medical treatment, and a great number of people among families of the deceased were hospitalized due to mental illness or the danger of suicide attempts. When we met with the director of the Department of Health, we told him that churches could help those people. He agreed with us wholeheartedly and confessed that despite the effort of the Department of Health, more and more people were committing suicide. We returned to Cheng Du after signing a written agreement to help the disabled people by cooperating with the director of the city. On our way back to Cheng Du, we received a phone call.

The call was an invitation from the president of a medium-sized company in Y city, which is not too far away from the site of earthquake. She said that she was deeply touched by the diligence of churches that came from afar to help the victims of the Sichuan earthquake. She also said that she would like to hear about the Gospel when we visited her. When we arrived at her company, we were surprised by two things. One was a wonderful building and a beautiful water fountain as well as a garden. Another was the 22 executive members waiting for us in the conference room. I told our party to take out the Bibles we had with us; there were a total of 11 Bibles. I distributed each of the Bibles to two people to share.

Since I didn't speak the local dialect, I began to explain the Gospel in Pekingese. At first the people had a hard time understanding my unfamiliar pronunciation, but with the help of the party's prayer and the Holy Spirit, they quickly got used to it. Finally, of the 22 participants that day, 21 people accepted Jesus Christ as their Savior.

A SPECIAL OFFERING FOR THE SICHUAN EARTHQUAKE

After the Sichuan earthquake, we made a special offering to help those who had been afflicted. Because the Chinese place great emphasis on money, I did not bring up the topic. However, the scope of the Sichuan tragedy demanded everyone's help and participation, so I sent out the message a week ahead of time and gave everyone an envelope to bring in their offerings the following week. The next week 25 people gave their offerings, which totaled to a thousand dollars. This was much more than I expected, considering our small church. I was curious as to who contributed the most, so I asked a finance committee member to bring me a list of the offerings. After careful review, I found out that a sister of our home church offered 400 dollars alone, so I brought her in privately and asked her how she was able to do what she did. Her answer was, "A while ago, when you were preaching, you said that the first fruit is for God and that you gave your first salary entirely as an offering to God. That's what I wanted to do so I offered my first paycheck after graduating from college." I was emotionally moved and gave her a prayer of blessing.

From the Bible's sowing parable I had believed that good soil was impossible to find or even non-existent and that there was only thorny bushes or rocky places. However, looking at the people I met in China, I was sure that I had found good soil. Their belief was so pure and clean that frequently I felt that I was there to learn from their loyal faith, rather than to preach the gospel. They were indeed the roots of happiness and encouragement for us.

VISITING THE KOREAN CHURCHES

We went on our first visit to Korea in more than two years during our children's school break. Of the several reasons we had for going, the most important was that my 84-year-old mother had been hospitalized with a cerebral infection. As soon as we arrived in Korea, my family and the home church leaders went straight to the hospital to pray for her. In spite of her age, she was recovering well, and by the time we returned to China, she was up and walking around.

The second reason we went was because the Korean missionaries who were working in Japan had requested that I lecture at a seminar. I had the opportunity to lead a four-day seminar on effective cross-cultural missions in Tokyo. On Sunday I preached at a Chinese worship service within a big Korean church of Tokyo, and it was personally a great blessing and inspiration. I was overwhelmed when I was told that the 240 Chinese believers had been praying for a week to hear preaching in Chinese. Until then there had only been Korean missionaries preaching in Korean or Japanese whose preaching then had to be interpreted into Chinese.

The third reason for our visit was to give the Chinese church leaders an opportunity to visit Korean churches. In China, churches do not get much recognition. To them church is just a place where people sing a few quiet hymns and listen to short sermons. Sometimes I could feel the limitations of what I could teach in theory. I wanted to tell them that the church was more meaningful than what they thought and provide them with the opportunity to discover the vision and direction for the future growth of Chinese churches. That is why I decided to take some of our home church leaders to Korea. Everyone had to pay for their own expenses and only those who were eligible to get a visa were allowed to participate. The Nanum church in Korea provided transportation, accommodation and other necessities so we were able to visit many churches in Korea during our stay without much difficulty. I was thankful to the Nanum church for the support they extended to our home church leaders and to my family.

We spent eight valuable days together and visited many different types of Korean churches, from a newly developing church with only 25 members to small churches of 200 and 3,000 members to some of the largest churches in the world with 40,000, 60,000 and 700,000 members. The reception staff from all the churches we visited welcomed our team and gave a detailed presentation of their church's vision and mission. This trip allowed us a time of learning, challenges and thankfulness. In addition, we visited E-land Company and through their presentation we were amazed to see how Christian corporations were actively working for the kingdom of God.

In the report that was submitted after their trip, the home church leaders wrote that they had realized the direction for Chinese churches and about the devotion, passion and servant mentality of Korean churches. To those who were raised as an only child at home, it was more difficult to be considerate of others, to sacrifice and to serve others with love as taught in the Bible. To them the love and servant leadership shown by Korean churches was truly inspiring.

Returning from Korea, there were a few changes in their religious life. Their perspective of sermons, the church and their awareness and recognition of missions changed. For example, they started to decorate their offices, which were used as places of worship: they made a stand for the preacher and decorated the church with flowers. In addition, they became more conscious of God's presence and increased their offering to support evangelists and relief efforts. I have no doubt that the Holy Spirit was leading our team. I have included more details about this trip, and our team's impressions and the insights they gained at the end of this book (Appendix B).

The fourth reason for visiting Korea was for our health examinations. Our health was deteriorating fast and my wife was feeling extreme tiredness every day. After my wife's health examination, we found out that there was a 0.9 cm-wide lump in her thyroid gland, so she went in for a re-examination. Our departure had to be delayed for a week, but we had complete faith that God would cure all our illnesses. Thankfully, the results showed that there was nothing serious about her health and that it was just a lump similar to a mole on the surface of the skin. The doctor told us to return for another examination after a year, and so we went back to China. Upon her return she no longer felt the tiredness she felt before, and I believe that God cured this, too, because our one-month stay in Korea was even more tiring than our work in China. Through this we came to have complete faith and belief that God was always with us, taking care of our family.

THE BEIJING OLYMPICS

The Olympics have a very special meaning to me. I was living in Seoul during the 1988 games; in Birmingham, which is only two hours away from Atlanta, during the 1996 games, and in Beijing during the 2008 games. I thought that going to watch the Beijing Olympics would be meaningful for the children, too, so I took them to watch a couple of Korean games. We could only get the tickets to see the women's hockey and baseball (Korea vs. Cuba), but the children were excited beyond expectation.

There were quite a lot of impressive moments during the Olympic games. The Korean teams performed well, especially the gold medal win in baseball. There were eight gold medals won by Michael Phelps, including 6 world records. However, the most impressive yet shocking moment was during the men and women's relay race by the American team. When everyone thought that the gold medal was theirs, both the men and the women's team runners accidentally dropped the relay baton. The results came out and their four years of hard work ended up fruitless, because they did not even get the bronze medal. Watching the games, I could feel the similarity between our beliefs and the running of a race.

Just as the author of the book of Genesis listed Abraham's God, Isaac's God and Jacob's God in the order of belief, in the New Testament, Paul compares one's belief to a race. It needs to be appropriately passed down from generation to generation. It is not simply about believing in Jesus and God during our lives, but it is about passing that faith on to our sons and grandchildren to glorify the almighty God. We need to make sure that our faith is clearly passed on to the next generation. In addition, there can only

Beijing

Beijing

Chong Ching City

Flowers for the worship service

Chong Ching Church

Church decorations

be a reward upon completing the race, and I realized the importance of team ministry. From this perspective we can say that our family and church are like a relay team.

CHRISTMAS IN THREE CITIES

It had already been three-and-a-half years since my family came to China. We had been focusing on spreading the gospel, nurturing leaders and urban missions. By the grace of the Lord, churches were built one after another and leaders were raised and sent to other regions. As a result, we were able to experience Christmas celebrations in three different cities; Beijing, Chong Ching, Guang Jo.

My wife and I wanted to visit the mission fields that we had developed together for the past few years. However, we could not because we had to take care of our three children, and we couldn't afford the plane tickets due to the sudden economic downturn — it was more expensive to fly within China than to fly to Korea. We couldn't even talk to our supporting churches for the needs because the economic downturn had also left them in difficult financial situations. But then my mother and father-in-law got to visit China for a month. They took care of our children, and we were able to purchase plane tickets for me, my wife and our son Segi with the support of our families in Korea.

The first Christmas celebration we went to was held in Beijing. I baptized 10 brothers and sisters after the Sunday service and they were delighted like children. Then we headed to a restaurant where the Christmas celebration was to be held. The venue was filled with 130 people from four different small churches, including some new faces I was not acquainted with. I felt like a stranger because I had not been able to visit the churches much while concentrating on training leaders.

Chinese leaders from different churches took the main roles in all events as usual. A young couple, who had played Mary and Joseph and used a doll for Jesus the year before, had their two-month-old son that year, which delighted the crowd. All the events were well-organized and filled with songs, dances and testimonies about the gospel.

Looking at the crowd, I thought of the time I had arrived in China and wondered, "Will I be able to evangelize one person here and share the gospel in Chinese? Will I be able to make use of the materials that I've prepared for 10 years in the U.S.?" I thought of the times when I was very discouraged and timid. It was surprising to see what the Lord had done in just three years.

During the Christmas event in Beijing, one of our sisters, Joo, and her husband gave a testimony of their experience with God. My wife had a prayer session every semester (excluding vacation time in consideration of their children) and Joo attended the session. She looked sad, so when my wife asked why, she replied that her daughter was sick. It turned out that her daughter had leukemia and needed a blood transfusion from the hospital. She also had a serious case of skin irritation that made sleeping at night difficult. She had a bandage wrapped around her arms and at my wife's inquiry, she explained that an unknown skin disease was spreading on her hands, arms and legs. Her skin looked more like tree bark rather than human skin. I heard later that her husband even presumed their daughter was suffering from leprosy. My wife quickly called me into the room and asked me to pray for her health. I was not used to praying with the purpose of healing people and hesitated momentarily, but convinced myself that I should give her some comfort by praying for her health.

I told her three things while looking into her eyes, so desirous to escape from these miserable days of her life. The first was that I did not have the power of healing. Secondly, as the Bible says, I told her Jesus healed the sick and always ended by saying "Your faith has saved you," so it was imperative to believe that God has the power to heal. Lastly, thinking of the apostle Paul, in spite of his strong faith and performing many miracles, I told her that God did not accept his ardent prayers for removing the thorns in his body. "I am an incomparably insignificant person compared to Paul, so how can I assure you that I can help you of this serious disease?" I said. As I spoke these words, I could sense that she was surprised and was slowly turning to despair. I continued by telling her that if her disease continued even after my prayer, that she was not to despair and should remember 2 Corinthians 12:9, 10. Even though Paul's sickness did not get better after praying to God, his faith grew stronger.

However, I told her that if God hears our prayers and cures us of our sickness, that is entirely the work of the Holy Spirit. So if she were healed, she should thank and praise only God and testify about this experience for the rest of her life. Then the sister asked us to visit her house and to pray for her daughter who was suffering from leukemia. So I said, as in the centurion's case, God will hear and respond to our prayer whether we are here or at her house. I laid my hands on her head and prayed for her.

One week later, I had to run an errand so I came home late. As soon as I walked into the house, my wife came running towards me shouting with excitement that Joo's daughter had been healed. Her physician said that she was fine so she need not go to the hospital again. Afterward, Joo and her husband evangelized 15 other people and were trained in how to plant a home church.

Our second Christmas celebration took place in Chong Ching, a big city with a population of over 30 million (Beijing has about 14 million), but it looks smaller than Beijing when you actually visit the city. I flew to Chong Ching with my wife and Segi. Segi was happy to be on the plane with just the three of us. Although Segi was only 10 years old, I wanted him to see and feel what it was like to be on the mission field from an early age. Segi still didn't know what exactly his parents did. We never told our children what we did because they would tell the truth when elevator guides, who were stationed in nearly every building in China, asked them about their parents' jobs. Instead, I told my children that I worked for a company (I actually had a 'vice president' title in a Chinese firm), but I also told them that I taught about Jesus to help people believe Jesus better and that all Christians do as I do. Segi would sometimes surprise me by asking, "What exactly do you do? Where is your office? What's your title? Why did you not go to work today?"

I prayed in silence in the plane, looking forward to the miracles the Lord would do in Chong Ching. It took us two-and-a-half hours to get there, but a warm breeze and green trees welcomed us. The wife of Professor J, who was the leader of the Chong Ching church, met us. Two months before, the couple had visited us in Beijing for a week to complete the first part of their training. After they got back to Chong Ching, the number of their church members increased to 28 within two months as a result of their hard work. It was fascinating. The new members were young, either college students or students who had studied abroad. Both my wife and I held retreats and prayer meetings every night during the three days of our stay. Every night we experienced the miracles of the Holy Spirit just as the Korean churches had experienced earlier.

Young believers filled a hotel room, concentrated on God's words, repented, rejoiced, found solutions and came back again the next evening with high hopes. My wife led the prayer meeting for an hour-and-a-half and I taught for two hours every night. She had people write the list of sins they had committed and then pray for repentance. As in Romans 8:1-2, we let them know that there is no condemnation for those who are in Christ Jesus and that we all can run to the throne of God by the grace Jesus has given us. They rejoiced in the freedom and peace they obtained through this repentance and deep understanding of the gospel. One person testified that he'd never felt this kind of joy and peace in his life.

On Sunday, I baptized nine people. Then I moved to a newly opened café where the Christmas celebration was to be held. God showed us His faithfulness and prepared a safe venue whenever we looked for one to hold such events. Church members bought the tickets, and their friends got free admission. About 60 people took part in the first Christmas celebration of the Chong Ching church. Professor J led all the programs. Some events were in English, because most of the church members were taking English Bible study classes. The venue was beautifully decorated, leaving us with a fresh impression and warm memories. Although no one was determined to believe Jesus on that day, 11 people raised their hands to know more about Jesus. Mrs. J wrote down their names and phone numbers to meet and tell them the good news later.

After leaving Beijing to head towards Chong Ching, I was somewhat tense and nervous. But with God's protection and grace, everything in Chong Ching went better than expected. So when it was time for us to head to Guang Jo, I was excited and expectant. The leader of the Guang Jo church greeted us at the airport. I had trained her for a year-and-a-half and she did quite well in an extremely difficult leadership training course. She had graduated with a degree in Chinese from Beijing University and was a journalist for the Economy section of the newspaper. Most of all, she was extremely passionate in spreading the gospel. She evangelized to over 90 people during the course of one year.

The temperature in Guang Jo was very warm. It was -8°C (18°F) when we left Beijing but when we got to Guang Jo, it was 20°C (68°F) . Beautiful flowers were blossoming alongside the road on our way into the city from the airport, and I came to realize that China was really a huge country. We had a special interest in Guang Jo for strategic reasons. The city was growing rapidly, with approximately six million inhabitants in the city and 30 million in the outskirts of the city. Guang Jo is also the center of trade in the southern part of the country, only about an hour and 40 minutes away from Hong Kong. The city's geographical location was of great strategic importance in spreading the gospel within China. Some people traveled three hours to come to Jao-Yang church in Beijing, and about half of the people traveled an hour-and-a-half to come to our church. Considering this, the fact that Hong Kong was only an hour and 40 minutes away from Guang Jo meant that in case of an emergency we could leave China and yet continue to train Chinese leaders. This made Guang Jo a strategically important city for us.

The Guang Jo church had the most number of people at 70. The interesting fact was that almost all the employees of a Chinese restaurant run by a sister named Lee became Christians, and then the restaurant became a church. Lee offered her whole house to serve our needs. The house was in a quiet location and it felt as if we were on vacation abroad. Each room had a mosquito tent because there were so many mosquitoes. Everything was fine until Satan started to challenge us at the baptismal ceremony. Originally, all 52 employees were to be christened. However, only three showed up for the ceremony. None of the three was an employee of the restaurant. I was stunned and could not understand. With a grim apologetic expression, the leader told us that Satan had convinced a few people to reject the baptism and that the others had followed the few. I performed the ceremony convincing myself that there was hope for the city as long as I could help change these three people.

The Christmas event that we had in Guang Jo on Christmas Eve was unlike any other Christmas event I had been to. It felt nothing like Christmas. The first reason was that it was warm, although it was winter. The second reason was that the event took place in broad daylight, which lessened the Christmas feeling. I wondered what a Christmas celebration would be like in the tropical equatorial cities, where it is constantly humid and hot. The third reason was the way the event became more of a talent show and company celebration because over 80 percent of the participants were employed by the restaurant. This was evidence to me that the Guang Jo church was untrained and lacked organization. A sense of responsibility and ownership, necessary if the church was to grow strong and thrive, had not taken root among the church members. I was certain that this was where the strong church that God wanted had to be built.

The day after the Christmas event, we had a four-day retreat just like in Chong Ching. Because the leader there was in her fifties, many in the congregation were senior citizens. Most were quite cynical and stubborn after having survived the infamous Cultural Revolution. These characters frequently bickered among themselves. There was also the problem of language. We spoke Mandarin while they were mostly accustomed to using Cantonese. Because of this, some could not fully understand the lecture and we had to stop intermittently to help everyone understand. But then, during my wife's praying session, people started to confess their sins, were forgiving others and praising God. My wife prepared food and served dinner. I gave a lecture based on the Bible, and from their facial expressions, I could see that they were beginning to focus on God's words.

Then, after having been blessed during the retreat, everyone would all go back home and fight with and criticize one another throughout the rest of the day, then return to the retreat and repeat the whole process all over again. I asked them the reason for their strange behavior. I realized that the main reason was that they did not think their leader was genuinely being transformed by Christ. The leader's friends in her hometown did not recognize the changes that were happening to the leader after believing in Jesus. This was in line with the saying in the Bible that a prophet is not well respected in his hometown.

The day before leaving Guang Jo, I thought of the Apostle Paul and his teaching on love. I felt that in order for the church to flourish, the members of the congregation ought to be free to remain or leave. I advised the leaders to let the people choose as they wanted and to restructure the organization of the church. After that the church was divided into two: a church for the younger generation and another for the older. Thankfully, both of these churches grew at an impressive speed.

OUR FIRST FURLOUGH

Before I left for China for the first time, I mentioned in a sermon that I was "going to break a rock with an egg." Indeed, it felt like that in my heart. However, when I look back at the first term now that four years have passed, I realize how great God's grace has been and how wonderful the first term was in comparison to my initial expectations.

It took us six months to prepare for our first furlough. We planned for the furlough in gratitude to God and prayed for it. My plans included recharging myself, resting, traveling with family, taking some classes with my wife in seminary, and enrolling my children at a Korean school. My wife and children were so excited that they couldn't asleep. We felt happy thinking about meeting our friends and church members whom we had not seen for four years. The anticipation of returning home made me feel like I was walking on the air.

Our family and local fellow workers had a great farewell party. During the party, I showed ministry pictures and videos of our four years in China. There was an outflow of grace, awe and gratitude among us. We praised the Lord and prayed for each other and churches in the Holy Spirit.

On August 11, 2009 we returned to Korea. We spent the first two months catching up with and enjoying friends and family. And we traveled everywhere we wanted to go. After this, we settled into "normal" life in Seoul. A Korean church which had a great interest in China missions offered us a small apartment. Our children enrolled in a nearby school. Though there was some re-entry shock, it was not a big problem because we had already trained well for moving and adjusting into a new environment.

While in Korea, we were able to visit churches and take care of church members in China every three months. When I left China, I gave each one of the church leaders homework such as evangelism, planting a church, starting small groups, or reading the entire Bible. I was able to check their monthly homework completion online and went to China every three months to give a hand. In addition, we returned to China during Christmas time, baptized people, and had a great time.

CHRISTMASTIME VISIT TO CHINA

Prior to visiting our church plants over Christmastime, my wife and I had two concerns. First, in the midst of economic difficulties, we had to decide whether I would go alone or take the family with me. We also had to decide whether it was a good idea to bring children with us when the A1H1 virus was prevalent.

While praying and seeking His guidance together, God reminded us of the delightful people we met the previous summer during our family's visit to the churches. The people at the church were surprised to see a Christian family like us, and one member told us that he felt challenged to have a Christian family of his own. Finally, God led us to make a decision to take this journey with our whole family based on the belief that it would be a good opportunity for the children. However, my concern regarding my

4-year-old daughter Grace would not go away, so we went to the hospital to get a vaccination against the A1H1 virus only to be turned down as we were late in making reservations. We would not be able to get vaccinated until early January.

We asked ourselves several questions. What were we going to do if A1H1 were to be around chronically? Were we going to continually stay at home and avoid going to places where people gather? What are we going to do if a disease worse than A1H1 spread in Beijing and somebody had to spread the Gospel to dying people? Is it wise to step back and cower when we face hardship? Finally, we came to a conclusion. This was our calling from God. Who are we and for what have we been called by God? We were missionaries called by God to spread the Gospel. Once we came to this conclusion, our future actions became clearly defined.

I honestly did not expect much from the Christmas service at the churches in China because I had been away for six months, which prevented me from encouraging and taking care of the churches like I used to. I actually worried that the leaders would have been so discouraged that the churches might have closed. I went with low expectations, determined just to baptize and encourage the members of the churches. But my wife thought differently. She thought this trip should be more than a chance to see church members and friends, considering the financial burden we had taken on and the risk we had taken with our children's health. She sincerely prayed and expected that people would be saved during the Christmas season and made the same prayer requests to several prayer supporters.

I was surprised to see my children so delighted upon our arrival to China. They even enjoyed our small room and the cold weather. In contrast, my wife and I were complaining about the cold weather and many other things. However, the amazing thing was that the Holy Spirit was clearly telling us what we should do and how we were going to do it as soon as we landed in China. We were filled with new strength and power and we thought this was the answer to our supporters' intercessory prayers.

We were accompanied by a Chinese brother we used to nurture. Our first visit was to Chong Ching Church, which was two hours away from Beijing by plane. Professor J, the church leader, served us wholeheartedly, and we thanked God and blessed him for everything that had been perfectly prepared.

Before I had gone on furlough, I had challenged the leader of the

Chong Ching church to establish a new church downtown by the time I came back. I couldn't thank God enough to see that the establishment was actually in progress. That night, I led a special worship at the new church. It was different to see five older members at the new church since the Chong Ching church is mostly comprised of young people. I preached from the Gospel of John for an hour-and-a-half on the topic of the Lordship of Christ and the kind of Christians God wants today.

ANOTHER CHRISTMAS IN CHONG CHING

God prepared a perfect place for us when we prayed for a safe place for the Christmas service. It was a hotel that had not yet been opened, and all the furniture was clean and new. Every time we had anxiously prayed for a safe place to hold a Christmas service, God always answered in an amazing way. At the Christmas service, there was a play that began with the Creation and ended with the gospel, accompanied by touching hymns. Six invited people accepted Jesus as their savior that night, and my three-day visit to Chong Ching ended with my baptizing four members who already completed the fundamentals courses.

Upon leaving the city, I encouraged the leader of the church and his wife to reflect the words of God in their everyday lives and set an example for the church members since the personal lives of the leaders would get more and more attention as time went by.

ANOTHER CHRISTMAS IN GUANG JO

It was in the middle of spring when we arrived in Guang Jo. I could see pink flowers by the road, which reminded me of the vastness of the country. The next day was Sunday and I led the daytime service. There were some new members among the 25 people gathered in the small room. There were also sister Jang's parents-in-law, who had been in her prayers for a long time. They accepted God as their Savior with my wife's daring invitation, and so did sister Sie's boyfriend who had come to worship for the first time. Liu, who had accompanied us from Beijing, led the prayers of acceptance and it must have been a blessing for him.

I remember what Jang's father-in-law said that day, after the acceptance prayers. "I know an old man who is over 100 years old, and I looked up to him since he is always calm and peaceful unlike me. He turned out to be a

Christian." I again realized that how important it is for Christians to set a good example to testify Jesus in our everyday lives.

The next day, my wife took time to counsel and pray for the church leader. She was still tormented by horrible memories from the times of the Cultural Revolution. According to her, bad people stormed in and took everything away including her parents and furniture. She and her two sisters hid until dark and had to live as poor orphans. People kept picking on her and she couldn't do anything to save her mother from all the criticism and insults.

She had been afraid and distrustful of people since the Cultural Revolution (1966-1976) when people were accusing one another. My wife wept with her and comforted her, telling her that God does not condemn us and loves us no matter what we have done. They prayed with all their hearts, hand in hand, asking God to free her from Satan's accusing shackles. She confessed and repented of her sins. The Holy Spirit mended her wounded heart with freedom and forgiveness, turning her into a brighter person from then on. I was told later that she evangelized 21 people in two weeks.

The Christmas service was held at a hotel restaurant in Guang Jo. I was a little disappointed to see many members missing. Later I found out that Christmas had overlapped with a traditional holiday and many who had unbelieving family members gave up coming to the church to keep the peace in their household. Thirty people attended the service, including the ones who left during the service. Two ladies who were baptized that day read 1 Corinthians 13 in a loud voice. Then our family sang and Grace played the angel on the stage, and it made everyone laugh and enjoy the service. Compared to the Christmas service in Chong Ching, there were many things that needed to be improved, but everyone at the service was delighted and touched. God really looks at the intent of the heart, unlike we do.

We had a lot of fun afterwards taking photos with our children. People were much more open to us because of them. If we had not brought them with us, we wouldn't have been able to earn their trust in such a short period of time. A lady came and asked my wife if she really was an actress from Korea, and others seriously asked me how to build this kind of happy and caring family. My wife answered, "The only secret is to depend solely upon God and put His words into practice in our everyday lives."

Even the church members who saw me for the first time showed sincere

97

respect for me and thanked me for sharing the gospel. I realized they were indeed members of the true church and felt ashamed of myself that I had always drawn lines between us. That night, the Holy Spirit filled everyone's heart and no one wanted to leave the place. Six out of the seven invited people accepted Jesus as their Savior, and eight individuals were baptized.

After we got back to Beijing, the leader reported to us that many young church members had decided to marry someone who would do God's work in the future so they can build a Christian family like ours.

CHRISTMAS IN BEIJING AGAIN

We got back to Beijing only to find the church there unprepared for the Christmas service. The leader had been too preoccupied with other work. We were disappointed and upset with them. "How could they have been less disciplined than other leaders despite the fact that they have spent more time with us than anybody else?" I was shocked to see them so unorganized and insensitive, considering that they had been the most spiritual leaders six months ago.

I rebuked them a little for this, and they clearly showed their displeasure with me. I was shocked again and couldn't say a word. Without resting, we began to prepare for the Christmas service scheduled for the next day with other members until 2 am. The worst part was that the service would be held during lunchtime because the reservation had been made too late. I was worried that many members would have to work and miss the service, and I also repented of blaming others for this unpreparedness. I sincerely prayed that at least one person would accept Christ through the Christmas service.

The next day, fifty people attended the service, which was beyond my expectations, and one person confessed Jesus as his personal savior. I really enjoyed singing and spending some meaningful time together with the leaders from other church groups. Nevertheless, I felt that there were still some leadership issues that needed to be addressed. I thought that the church leaders were not humble because they had not been able to learn from us. I repented and prayed, and God comforted me with the fact that He is glorified not only through my success but also through my failures.

We sent gifts to the cleaning company again, which had become our annual event. We had things to be thankful for every year ever since we began pampering this company five years ago. Some people want fruits without even sowing the seeds, and others expect to harvest much more than they have sowed. In this sense, sending gifts to cleaning companies was a true inspiration from God. Forty-five people had become Christians through our outreach over the past four years.

There were only two people in the office when our church team brought the gifts to them. My wife was a little disappointed, but this turned into a good opportunity to have a long conversation with the president who told my wife to come back again in the morning to speak to more people.

The next day, my wife went with a sister whom she had trained. Twenty-two people were waiting for them. My wife first explained the meaning of Christmas, and then sister C shared the gospel for 25 minutes. When invited, ten people raised their hands to accept Jesus as their Savior. They prayed for the ten people that very morning, and we had a chance to train them a week later.

My wife came back home with a blushed face and told me, "Even right after experiencing the amazing work of the Holy Spirit, I was afraid of policemen who might follow me." She also told me that she had walked around the marketplace to get away from some suspicious-looking men. She looked timid, but God was using her. I thought of a story that D. L. Moody had told. One day, after preaching, an intelligent-looking young man criticized him. "It was a good sermon, but I was uncomfortable with your wrong choice of grammar and vocabulary from time to time." Moody replied with a smile, "I know I have many flaws, but what else can God do other than using someone weak like me? Since smart people like you are not committed…"

I realize again that God uses us not because we are smart and special, but because we have been saved by His grace. God would be more than delighted to fulfill his plans if better Christians devoted themselves to Him.

NEW YEAR'S EVE IN CHINA

We attended the first New Year's Eve service at the new church building in Beijing. Twenty-five people gathered and prayed, sang, worshiped and even watched a movie. We were filled with joy and the Holy Spirit. We picked the words of God by drawing lots. In the Bible, there were times when people asked God's will by drawing lots when making important decisions (Judges 1:1), for tracking down the suspects (Jonah 1:7), and when establishing the leader of the churches (Acts 1:26). We carefully

99

selected 100 verses, and each of us picked three times. We also wrote five prayer requests and made a copy — we each kept one and then shared the other so we could pray for each other in the coming year and see how God answered our prayers a year later.

I received three stern verses. Reading the words again and again, I realized that God wanted my ministry and life to be of higher quality.

These are the 3 verses I picked:

Matthew 6:4 – "...so that your giving may be in secret. Then your Father, who sees what is done in secret, will reward you."

1 Timothy 4:7 – "...rather, train yourself to be godly."

1 John 4:20 – "If anyone says, 'I love God,' yet hates his brother, he is a liar. For anyone who does not love his brother, whom he has seen, cannot love God, whom he has not seen."

My wife picked:

1 Samuel 16:7 – "But the LORD said to Samuel, 'Do not consider his appearance or his height, for I have rejected him. The LORD does not look at the things man looks at. Man looks at the outward appearance, but the LORD looks at the heart'."

Isaiah 40:31 – "...but those who hope in the LORD will renew their strength. They will soar on wings like eagles, they will run and not grow weary, they will walk and not be faint."

Matthew 6:33 – "But seek first his kingdom and his righteousness, and all these things will be given to you."

When my wife selected the verse from 1 Samuel, she knew that she had a tendency to judge people she met during her ministry by their appearances or their attitude. However, through these verses she hoped to see people's hearts from God's perspective. The other verses encouraged her to keep her focus on God and the cross as well as on spreading the gospel.

The verses selected provided many testimonies for others, too. Mahao, a brother serving a church in Sichuan's earthquake recovery site, chose two verses, James 1:19 and 1:20. These two verses were supposed to be together, but my wife mistakenly separated them into two pieces. During the first round, Mahao selected verse 19 and surprisingly, during the second round, selected verse 20. Even more surprising was that the women at the gathering mostly chose verses that applied to women and the men chose verses that applied to them.

At the New Year's prayer service that my wife was leading, there were members of the church who had not participated in the New Year's Eve gathering, so after the prayer service we drew lots again to select verses for them. My wife delivered a message concerning people's endless sin towards God, especially idolatry and lust, and repentance for disregarding the holy teachings of Jesus using Psalm 78:32-42, 1 Peter 1:13-17 and Romans 2:2-11. During the prayer service, there was one sister who was disturbing my wife. She seemed disinterested in praying, and when everyone else was praying she was watching them with her eyes wide open. After a long two-hour prayer service, my wife opened her eyes assuming that the sister would have gone home. However, to my wife's surprise she was still there. My wife was surprised but did not let it show and explained in detail the verses they had selected, telling them that the verses were given by God to bless their New Year.

Then the sister held up the verses she had picked and shouted, "This is amazing! This is just right! The verses are pointing out my problems!" The verses she had picked had to do with idolatry. She confessed that there was a Buddhist idol on one wall and a cross on the other in her home, and that she always prayed in fear looking at the cross or looking at both walls. Hearing this, my wife, the leaders of the group, and sister J told her that idol is nothing to be afraid of and went to her house to get rid of the idol.

My wife was first surprised to see the well-organized house and then surprised again to see a number of idols in the room. She was a former soldier. When they were about to get rid of all the idols, she said the idols were expensive and got upset, asking if she could give them to other people. The group leaders told her that the idols should be destroyed so that no one else would worship them. Brother C testified that he liked Harley Davidson so much that he had collected mini bikes almost worth a hundred thousand dollars, but that God provides us with better things when we give up on things that we love. She was happy to hear his testimony and got rid of all the idols. They prayed at all the corners of her house, and my wife encouraged her about the confidence and power that children of God have.

The next day, our brother Chun's wife Ting Ting called her to arrange a visit. My wife took along a hymn book, a CD, a light stand, Korean coffee, magnetic cards that said "Prayer Changes Things" and "God Loves You" and a pretty Korean sweater. She looked happy to see them and my wife asked her if she had a good night's sleep. She answered that she had a very comfortable night and promised Ting Ting that she would take part in the fundamentals course for the five coming weeks. They were filled with gratitude.

THE END OF OUR VISIT TO CHINA

The three fruits I gained through that last trip were: 32 Chinese coming back to the Lord, 16 Chinese baptized, and the beginnings of a church for artists. God truly makes everything happen in His time. I had prayed for many years and trained leaders to establish a church for celebrities and artists, but the results had been delayed.

Actress J, who had decided to commit herself to the church, apologized to me for not making up her mind earlier. After the first gathering, she joyfully wrote to me, "Although few people (four actors) attended our first worship service, we saw hope and the Lord's guidance. I, as the leader, could grow much more in faith than others. I regret that I did not commit myself earlier and really want to do my best to help the small group grow into a church. I thank God and you."

I had a candid conversation with the leaders of the Beijing church the night before I went back to Korea. The Holy Spirit worked in their hearts beforehand through the year-end events and worships. They repented of their arrogance and we reaffirmed our love and trust toward each other.

To be honest, I had a thought in the corner of my mind that it was our zeal that enabled us to plant four churches in China during the past four years. However, the Spirit proved that the "church is God's, and the Spirit works to establish it" while I was away from China. The Spirit founded six more churches during the eight month of our absence. It sounded like the Spirit was telling me that "the four churches planted in the past were also My (God's) Work." I repented of my attempt to steal God's glory for myself and glorified Him with thanks and praise.

As I reflected on God's goodness, He brought to mind what He had accomplished:

W. Shin

Type of church	Planted	In Process
General local church	✗	
Professors-centered church	✗	
Young people-centered church	✗	
2nd General local church	✗	
3rd General local church	✗	
Artists church		✗
Entertainers Church	✗	
General Church	✗	
Students Church		✗
Company Church		✗

Seven of these churches were completed before January 2011. In addition, for two years, we were part of the leadership team that planted the Japanese and International Churches.

SEVEN QUESTIONS' ACTUAL APPLICATION FOR CHINA MISSIONS

1. Home Church: How can we help to grow each home church into a healthy church that harmonizes a healthy faith, theology and life?
• Pioneer churches
• Nurture local leaders
• Build a church network

2. Creative Ministry: How can we create and develop new ministries while securing and maintaining current business at the same time in the midst of quickly changing world?
• Oh! Oh! Bible Study—creative new Bible study method
• Apples of Gold—creative new Bible study class for women focusing on building healthy families
• Evangelism—creative new evangelical method
• Special nurturing—creative new nurturing method
• Discipleship—creative new evaluating method
• New approach—building and using relationships
• Counseling—for depression, marriage and family matters

3. Governmental Ministry: How are we going to work with the government to become more Christian-friendly?
- Look for the needs of the government and people
- Abide by the laws set by the government
- Establish training center for Christian businessmen and CEOs
- Present thesis papers on how Christians can contribute to society

4. Patriot Church Ministry: How can we help the 15 million members of the Three-Self Church (三自 Three-self：自传-self-propagating and -teaching，自养-self-supporting，自治-self-governing) take on the responsibilities of the church?
- Cooperation through fellowship among businessmen and CEOs
- Cooperation between international churches
- Cooperation between various ministries and nurturing their leaders

5. Ministry of Alienated Group: How are we going to serve those who are neglected?
- Orphanages
- Poor people
- Handicapped people
- Meet their various needs and supply them with Bibles

6. Minority Ministry: How can we effectively spread the gospel to 55 different races who adhere to various religions?
- Support theology school for minority race
- Support training facilities for minority race
- Nurture Christian leaders of minority race
- Support other necessities
- Make and build a road

7. World Mission Participation: How can we get Chinese churches with a total of 90 million saints involved in world missions?
- Dispatch and support home church missionaries
- Support for the Mission of the fellowship among Christian businessmen
- United ministry with Overseas Chinese church

CONCLUSION

We experienced God's goodness and faithfulness during our first term. We are guided by the Holy Spirit to share the gospel, nurture leaders, build churches and serve people. The churches that we have planted belong to God and He will eventually fulfill the vision He gave us according to His will, using His ways, and through our faith and submission. Our job is to thank and praise Him, continuously preach the gospel, and put His Word into practice in our everyday lives with perseverance.

Shout for joy to the LORD, all the earth. Worship the LORD with gladness; come before Him with joyful songs. Know that the LORD is God. It is He who made us, and we are His; we are His people, the sheep of His pasture. Enter His gates with thanksgiving and His courts with praise; give thanks to Him and praise His name. For the LORD is good and His love endures forever; His faithfulness continues through all generations. — Psalm 100:1-5, a psalm of thanksgiving

I thank God for calling and using us to serve the Chinese people. I love China and the Chinese people because I love Jesus.

May 2011 – Beijing

APPENDIX A

APPLES OF GOLD MISSION STATEMENT

The primary purpose of Apples of gold is for older women to nurture younger women in the Word of God, the Bible, and to encourage them to obey that Word.

The program is based on the principles taught in Titus 2:3-5, which teach six ways to enhance our spiritual and personal lives, the lives of our family, and the lives of those around us.

The title of the program comes from Proverbs 25:11, which states: A word aptly spoken is like apples of gold in setting of silver. The secondary purpose of the program is the practical application of these principles:

- Cooking skills
- Relational skills
- Homemaking skills
- Sharing hospitality with others

(Betty Huizenga, 2000, p.10)

HOMEWORK REPORTS FROM APPLES CLASS

Hospitality – by Lina

What did you learn from today's lesson?

Thanks for the grace of Lord today, I've learned more principles of hospitality. Thanks for all the teachers and sisters in this training process, thank you for your serving. Thank you Mrs. Shin for showing me an example of hospitality. I have changed a lot through these 6 classes. I and my husband have changed and decorated our home to make it more hospitable, and we have also changed our attitudes towards and ways of treating our guests. Through the course today, I understand that the purpose of my home is to share the grace of Christ, which is just the very thing my heart desires and one of the things I really want to do in my life. How I wish that my home can be used by Lord to become a blessing to others day by day.

How will you apply and practice what you learned in your daily life?
I have always served many brothers, sisters and new friends in my home, but deep in my heart I know that I prefer to serve old friends and the ones I like. But from now on I also wish to use my home to serve more new friends and the ones who need Gospel. May the Lord help me to be a woman busy at home, kind and loving, to serve every guest as if serving Jesus. May the Lord give me strength so that my home can become a pipe of flowing blessings.

Any other suggestions or comments?
I am so thankful for the service of Mrs. Shin, it's a really heavy task. I know that she is often busy until midnight with preparations to serve us. She gives me a very good example of a wife/woman who conforms to the heart of the Lord. May our Lord bless this family who pour themselves out for God richly. My life has been changed greatly since I met Dr. Shin and his wife. Thank you for your service. I and my husband will try our best to imitate your example, the same way you imitate Christ.

Hospitality – by Yuan

What did you learn from today's lesson?
I gained a greater understanding of hospitality:
1. Hospitality is a command of the Bible.
2. Hospitality to guests is not only sharing our material things from God but also our lives and the Good News with them.
3. We should be the servant of our guests.
4. God blesses the person who welcomes others.
5. Hospitality flows from my faith in God.

How will you apply and practice what you learned in your daily life?
My family often welcomes some college students. I'd like my husband and I to have one heart, focusing on one ministry, giving everything we have to God, serving our brothers and sisters as servants, putting our faith in God and obeying His commands.

Any other suggestions or comments?

This Bible study has changed my views about the wife's role in a family, because God's Word has changed my heart.

Thank God for His boundless grace and this Bible study. I am grateful to my co-workers who worked hard.

I am grateful to Shin's family. They are the good example to me, especially Mrs. Shin. GOD BLESS YOU.

Kindness – by Li

What did you learn from today's lesson?

I appreciate this learning opportunity. The biggest lesson I learned today is to show kindness to myself, which I seldom do.

Kindness is a decision to obey the will of Holy Spirit.

Kindness is an attitude God shows to me so He would like me to show the same kindness to others.

The object of kindness could be anyone and everyone, even my enemy. I should show kindness to everyone and take no revenge on evil.

How will you apply and practice what you learned in your daily life?

Firstly, I should change my attitude to my husband. I am used to bossing him around and ignoring him, so kindness is my first challenge. Lord, please help me! Besides, I should show kindness to everyone and obey the guidance of the Holy Spirit.

Hospitality – by YQing

What did you learn from today's lesson?

1. Hospitality is God's command.
2. To serve guests shows our faith to God and our obedience to God's instruction. I'd love to share my home with others and be a servant.
3. Our house, and everything in it, is a gift from Lord. The real purpose for all the things He gives us is to share with others the love of Jesus Christ.

4. Before you make your guests (friends or strangers) feel at home and comfortable at your home, you should first of all make your own family members feel comfortable in it.
5. Do everything with your husband as a co-worker with one heart, pray together and consult with each other.
6. Hospitality is not only about food-sharing, but also life-sharing. I am grateful to our teacher today for illustrating to us the spiritual meaning behind hospitality.

How will you apply and practice what you learned in your daily life?
1. I have a new appreciation of the meaning of hospitality. I need to treat it with a godly and reverent attitude because it's the command of God.
2. Pray for Lord to consecrate my house, so that He can have supreme authority over my home.
3. To do hospitality with my husband with one mind, and pray together for that.
4. To imitate the "Lady Tidus", glorify the Lord's name in all circumstances.

Any other suggestions or comments?
The testimony our teacher shared today is really touching. The experiences that how she was entertained and how she and her husband entertain others help us a lot to understand the meaning of hospitality. Thank you teacher being such an example to us!

P.S. Mrs. Shin taught us via many ways and in many aspects to let us know how to serve through all these six classes. Thank you Mrs. Shin for dedicating your home to entertain us, and share your life and God's love with us.

Holiness – by YN

What did you learn from today's lesson?
Holiness is one of God's natures, and is His requirement to His people. But depraved men cannot rely on themselves to live a life of holiness. They

can only do so by the salvation of Christ, the guidance of the Holy Spirit and obedience to God's Word. How can a Christian live a life of holiness after he or she has been sanctified? He needs to live on God's Word, obey His will, and watch his mouth, eyes, feet and road according to His Word. In all things, he should look upon God and do His will, so as to glorify God with his holy life.

How will you apply and practice what you learned in your daily life?
Pray to God every day, beseech Him to cleanse me and protect my heart, mouth and feet, making every thought of my heart and every word of my mouth pure, so that my steps will not depart from God's ways.
Memorize God's Word, keeping His commandments in my heart.
Keep away from the things and environment of temptation.
Love my husband.

Submission – by Xiao

What did you learn from today's lesson?
This Bible study is exactly what I have needed. It has been very helpful. I learned five ways to express love to my husband and how to understand a man's needs. I thank God for giving me this course and a good class.

I realize that I need repentance, and that my husband has many needs. He needs my support and prayers very much. I learned that we should love each other. I should help him and be a good wife according to God's will.

How will you apply and practice what you learned in your daily life?
1. I should reflect on my attitude toward my husband.
2. Keep away from the tests and take care of my husband.
3. Love and accept my husband more, and understand his needs.
4. Express my love to him and welcome him in the first five minutes after he comes home every day, make our home neat and sweet so he could feel relaxed, delighted and comfortable.

Submission – by Lee J

What did you learn from today's lesson?

Thank God! As a Christian, what I learned mostly before was obeying God, but I learned today how to obey my husband. Through the Lord and in Him, I will. Please help me, Lord, and thank you, Lord, for giving me this Bible study because I learned a lot in every lesson.

Submission, all kinds of submission is based on submission to God.

Submission to men is very hard because humans are not perfect, but through fearing God, we can submit to men.

I should obey and exalt my husband in my marriage.

How will you apply and practice what you learned in your daily life?

Firstly, learn to obey my husband in the big and little things.

Teach my child to submit and be a good example for him through my submission to husband.

Submit to my mother-in-law.

Submit to my boss. When I find it hard to submit, I should know I have been crucified on the cross through Jesus, so I will not give in to anger.

Another lesson learned: A wife is a good soldier in family, so I should protect my husband and child.

APPENDIX B

The following the letters will give readers some creative ideas on how to continue relating with, discipling and training local fellow workers during furlough.

CHINESE FELLOW WORKERS' MISSION TRIP TO KOREA

On the Chinese Labor holiday in May, ten leaders of the Chinese home church visited Korea. The first purpose of the visit was to visit our family, and the second was to experience the Korean church. I willingly welcomed their visit because I really wanted them to know that the Church is bigger than they thought. They have only experienced small home churches in China, so they understood that church is just the place for prayer and worship only. This trip gave them a wonderful opportunity to envision possibilities for the Chinese church.

I was especially touched to spend time with my fellow workers in Korea. We went places together freely, praised God out loud, discussed God and our faith without having to be careful of the police and shared the gospel regardless of where we were. We were so grateful to God.

In the following paragraphs, I would like to present reports that my fellow workers wrote as they reflected on their visit to Korea and churches there.

Travel Report to Korea (by Tao, actor)

First of all, I would like to thank Pastor Shin, his wife and brother Chae for taking care of us for a week. To say just one more thing, all of you are truly living in the image of Jesus Christ. I have so many things to learn from you.

A true Christian's life is not for show on the surface but to grow internally. For the past seven days, Pastor Shin, his wife and brother Chae have worked hard to serve God and others, and to spread the gospel. Having experienced your servant heart, I am ashamed of myself. I thought of myself as a good and faithful servant of God, but after visiting Korea and meeting the Korean brothers and sisters, I realized the things I had been doing are so small.

The next thing I realized was the blessing that God has bestowed on the people of Korea. The moment I arrived in Korea, beginning at Incheon International Airport till we arrived in Seoul, I liked and envied the civility of the people, the environment of the country and the development of Seoul. I feel that China has a lot to learn from Korea.

The first day, as we made our way to Chungshin Church, I was shocked by the number of crosses on church rooftops. I truly felt that Korea was a country of the gospel and a Christian nation. People's well-being and kindness were considered blessings from God. I was able to witness the piety of the congregation as I entered Chungshin church. The church was solemn, and the interior design with two stories of seats versus one story in China was novel to me. The pastor preached on raising children, and pastors at other churches also mentioned children's education. The importance that Koreans place in spiritual training during childhood is the reason they instruct their children in the faith from a young age.

At Nanum Church, I was impressed by the way the saints served one another. Earnest, careful and voluntary service is truly a sign of Christ's love. Their praise team consisted of young people who were passionate and graceful. It made me want to praise God.

At Soon-Bok-Eum Church with 700,000 members, I realized how wonderful it was to have the world's largest church in Korea. This is proof of God's blessing. This is not only God's blessing on one church but also on the nation as a whole. Numerous people inside the church also amazed me. I had never seen so many Christians in my life. I thanked God. I was able to feel the power of prayer when everyone prayed out loud. Though I didn't understand what the pastor preached about, I was full of the Spirit. My heart, before and after the service, was different. I wanted to do something right then to spread the gospel in China.

We visited many churches while we were in Korea. Pastor Shin gave us a detailed explanation wherever we went. He was like a shepherd guiding us. He was full of joy and passion rather than fatigue and exhaustion. His passion and eagerness for spreading the gospel in China was transmitted to me. I hope that I too will have a heart like his.

Pastor Shin provided us with daily meals, clothes and lodging. He tried hard to make us feel at home in a foreign country. I felt like I was in China.

It was as if I was enjoying the happiness of a sunny spring day with my parents. I thank you.

I also had a touching experience at a prayer house. I was amazed at the sight of various towers and caves of prayer. I recommended to my Chinese friends to visit these places. Though my legs went numb and I was in tears, my heart was at peace, and my soul was not hungry at all. It was a very unique experience and a seminal point for the vision I received for a life dedicated to the gospel.

We all cried when pastor Shin saw us off at the airport. Parting from him and his wife was the hardest thing we did during the seven days of our stay. I can obey whatever it is that they want me to do, except for parting from them. I love Pastor Shin and his wife. They are my parents as well as my mentors in my heart. Moreover, they are my shepherd and my guide.

Visiting Korea was transformational for me. I decided to quit smoking. I became more concerned for others. My choice of acting projects to be involved in is now influenced by Scripture and I want God to use my acting gift to spread the gospel. Above all, my spiritual life has been purified; I realize what aspects of my life to dedicate to God in order to be used to share the gospel.

Travel Report to Korea (by Liu, home church leader)

I was impressed by Korea's cleanliness and orderliness. The gospel has not only developed the economy but the culture of the nation too. This made me more devoted to spread the gospel in China. This was God's grace upon me. Before I came to Korea, I was often disappointed by the Chinese people. After visiting Korea, I have become hopeful about China's future when the gospel is fully spread over the nation. I am committed to sharing the gospel more than ever.

I was greatly touched by how warm-heartedly Pastor Shin and his wife looked after us with care. In experiencing their devotion, I also decided to try harder to take care of others. I thought I already had the heart of serving others, but I realized I am yet to be like Pastor Shin and his wife. While observing Korean saints who took care of us generously, I also became aware that the Spirit's wonderful work. I should always pray about everything and obey the Spirit's guidance before serving, while serving and after serving people.

I became more desirous of God's words after I received an answer from God while praying on the Mountain of Prayer. I was also able to acutely experience the power of God's words. I became aware that there is nothing better than reading the Bible and praying to God. Pastor Shin always encourages me to be more passionate about reading the Bible and praying.

Lectures by the professors at Westminster Theological Seminary expanded my spiritual sight and strengthened my comfort, joy and determination to share the gospel. I am no longer afraid of the spiritual battle because I believe that the victory of the cross in Jesus Christ leads me to freedom. The professors were also great role models as they demonstrated humility, expertise and the leading of the Holy Spirit as they answered our questions. I realized that careful study of theology is important to the growth of my faith and my heart for serving the church.

The enormous size of the Korean church showed how widespread the gospel is in that nation. I truly respect the many missionaries who left their countries, families and friends, sacrificing their lives to spread the gospel in this land. I realized the need for respect and understanding of the missionary's life and mission. I also learned that Pastor Shin needs more protection from the people in China.

It was very precious to see children of God serving Him. I was so sure that God must be happy to see them worshiping Him selflessly and faithfully. Through my weakness, God's completeness comes through. I will not judge myself thoughtlessly. I will provide a shelter for brothers and sisters in Christ, serve them with love and a compassionate heart, and grow together with them.

I will be more devoted. I will live my life sincerely without any falsehood. My faith grew tremendously during the one year of obedience to God after I received His calling. This trip to Korea assured me. I am grateful to God for letting me realize that necessary preparatory work must be done for future churches in China. I want to be more holy, pure, diligent, and unrelenting with training myself. I will humbly learn and obey God's words and passionately share the gospel.

I truly appreciate Pastor Shin and his wife's looking after me, and I hope to always meet you in our prayers.

Graces I have received from visiting Korea (by Professor Sie, home church leader)

Serving: Beginning with their greeting at the airport, I was looked after by Pastor Shin's family and brother Chae. As I passed airport security, Pastor Shin's family welcomed me. I was very happy at this unexpected welcome, and it felt like I was at home. Did I really just arrive in a foreign country? It made me doubt where I was. Though my family was still in China, Korea didn't feel strange at all.

Service at Nanum church: Although not many people attended the service, it was one that was prepared with the heart of a home church. I was touched by the praise time and sermon prepared in Chinese as well as the thoughtfulness of the church members which came through in their prayers for us. It felt as if this church had always been my spiritual home. Tears ran down my cheeks. I asked Pastor Shin's wife if the sermon had been especially prepared for us, but she said no. However, I could tell that God had specially prepared this sermon for us through heartfelt prayers. Because my faith was weak, I was especially consoled and encouraged by the sermon.

I learned that God receives even my weakness. I am truly like an Israelite being trained in the wilderness. I'd always thought that God despised me for having a weak faith. I foolishly concluded that two-thirds of my life was filled with things that God disliked. However, I have now come to the realization that it is these two-thirds of my life that God is pleased with. God strengthens me when I am weak. God knows that I am a weak sinner, and He consistently helps me when I am weak. This is grace.

How can I fully fathom God's grace and use it all? Others have always mocked me for my foolishness and the slowness of my wings, like that of an eagle. Many people criticized me for taking such a long time to fly up. I didn't realize why the wings were necessary. I didn't understand why my wings weren't as agile and useful as those of others. However, the situation wasn't what I thought it to be. My wings allow me to fly higher and higher. I can fly up as high as 5,000 meters with the help of the wind of the Spirit. An eagle needs a long take-off distance and more time in order to fly high. Therefore, judging Christians to be foolish according to their outward appearance is in fact an incorrect judgment.

Pastor Kim, many deacons and a deaconess at Nanum church, were very kind and gracious to us. Their faith and service to me influenced me greatly. I was impressed with the associate pastors and male deacons who grilled meat in the heat, and the female deacons who cooked and distributed food compliantly. I was especially impressed with the way the white-haired deaconess greeted me. Her serving was a precious testimony to me because the older generation in China want to be served rather than to serve others. I realized from seeing her that those who serve others are the church. Those who serve others sincerely and truthfully are to be respected. This is what God wants from me.

Prayer: I learned the most when we visited a prayer house. In John 4:48, Jesus said, "Unless you people see miraculous signs and wonders, you will never believe." I was like that too, previously. I had seen God's work through many events, but I had not seen God in them. Such were my problems before coming to Korea. Of course I should believe in God, but my faith was lacking. God has done so many things in my life, and though I had heard many things through people's testimony, my faith was still weak. What will happen to me in the future? I was always uncertain and worried about it. Whenever I became aware of the condition of my faith, I felt uncomfortable. I struggled. I was always troubled because I could find no solution despite my effort.

However, I found the answer to my problem upon visiting the prayer house. Pastor Shin had specially prepared a structured time of prayer which consisted of a lesson, a break and 100 minutes of non-stop prayer. I prayed sincerely according to Pastor Shin's teaching and guidance. After prayer, I asked for God's answer and finally achieved my goal. I received an answer to my prayer and came to have faith in God. My struggles had been caused by my fear and lack of trust in God. I humbly committed my whole life to God.

God's answer has solved my problem appropriately at the right time. I realized how important prayer is and believed that God is always with me. God does not give His words to be a burden to me but to help me. I was at peace because I was able to hold God's hand through prayer whenever and wherever. I focused on praying and wanted to pray more because I knew to whom I was talking.

Missions: I saw many missionaries this time, sent out with the blessing of the churches. I was able to realize the true meaning of the church. Sharing the gospel is God's blessing. I witnessed a lot of God's blessing in Korea and the United States. The Chinese people must evangelize to bring this blessing into our lives.

Missions is God's work and needs the cooperative efforts of the church community. I saw several missionaries being sent out by Onnuri Church on their Wednesday night missions service. I also heard about various supporting works for missionaries such as providing materials, individuals' mission offerings, children' ministries, building churches, schools and hospitals, missiological business and so on. And I met a deacon who treated us to dinner, a medical doctor committed to missionary care, and two seminary professors who love China and world missions.

The spiritual growth of the leaders of the Chinese home churches is critical in spreading the gospel in China. Pastor Shin has put lots of efforts into doing this and has suggested solutions. I too believe that these solutions will solve the problem. We have to depend on God only, depend on the truth, and follow the Holy Spirit's guidance. We should bring the true gospel into China and the Chinese church for healthy churches to be founded. Through the gospel, China as well as the Chinese church can be revived.

Experience and application through the trip to Korea
by Ning (CPA), wife of Professor Sie.

From the moment I met Pastor Shin's family after passing through the airport security until I left Korea for China, my daily life was full of joy. Whenever I recalled the time I had in Korea, my eyes get teary.

I didn't feel awkward at all after arriving in Korea. Though the spoken language was different, sisters and brothers in Christ treated us like family. Even Pastor Shin's little children, Segi and Dan, took care of us. The second morning after our arrival, Segi and Dan made breakfast and coffee for us. Generally, I am very used to receiving guests, but I was being served by these little boys who were only about 10 years old. Pastor Shin and brother Chae drove us places, bought things for us, contacted places we were headed to, prepared our itinerary, translated and answered questions for us. Pastor Shin's lectures also filled up our spiritual needs once again.

My heart ached with sympathy for their lack of sleep. Pastor Shin's wife took care of us, her spiritual children, in addition to her own three children. I was ashamed of myself to see her like this. There is a saying that goes like this: "A woman in a new marriage is not able to volunteer because she just got married. Neither can she when has a baby to take care of, when the child is young and needs parenting, or when the child is a juvenile and needs the parents' support. When the woman is old and sick in bed, she is not able to volunteer, and she complains that God has not taken care of her health." However, this trip made me realize that serving is not to be done during certain seasons of one's life, but can be done whenever one has the heart. I prayed that I would serve others with such a heart of love.

1. Impression of church visit

a. I saw good-looking, young people dressed up, holding Bibles in their hands at the entrance to Chungshin Church. Though they seemed busy, they were in order. The image of Sunday morning at a Korean church was like that of a national holiday. People looked happy and peaceful; such countenance can only come from worshiping God. We do not worship God so that He wouldn't lose face or because it's an option in life. Worship must be the most important thing in our lives. These young people's worship was full of joy, wonder, and God's glory.

b. Nanum Church made me feel like I had returned home to China. Seeing the young people praising God on stage made me think how the future of the church depended on them. Saints receive service from these young people and are made aware of how God's love and care is different from that of the world's. I am not used to receiving warm hospitality because I have been taught to be self-reliant since I was young, and grew up receiving no help or care from others. According to a Chinese old proverb, there is neither love nor hatred without a reason. However, I learned that God's love is unconditional. Even though I had never met the young people who served me, their love and care captivated my cold heart.

c. Soon-Bok-Eum church was so big that it was like a masterpiece. It looked like a grand theater rather than a church. Though I didn't understand the sermon, I was impressed by the power of prayer when thirty thousand people all prayed out loud together. I realized that the prayers of a multitude can have a greater impact.

d. I realized that God has given a different vision to each church I visited. Our duty is to devote ourselves to God's mission.

2. Things I felt and learned

Pastor Kim's sermon about transcendence: People's thoughts are hard. When I am going through hardship, God's way prepared for me seems hidden. It seems God does not listen to my prayer. Because I think God doesn't show any interest in me or love me, I become disobedient to God. Instead, I count the reasons to criticize God for not helping me when I am in a trouble.

However, this is what God thinks. He is eternal, omnipotent, and never sleeps or is tired. Whatever He gives me, He has deemed to be the best for me. His wisdom is immeasurable, and his plan is perfect. He has the ability to achieve everything He wills. Likewise, He wants the best out of my life, too. Therefore, we should not limit our perspective to the circumstances and hardship that we are in, but trust God wholeheartedly. We should learn how to transcend our ego of the past. Although we are in pain and hardship, we must praise God. After the hardship comes God's blessing.

Clean Korea: The rest area we stopped at on our way to the East Sea was very clean. Foods were fresh and service was good. The seawater at Keong-Po beach was very pure; I could hardly see any garbage on the beach. The natural landscape was well preserved and the harmony between people and nature was clear.

After arriving at Seo-lak Mountain, I was even more impressed. I was born in northeast China, and the view in my hometown is very similar to that at Seo-lak Mountain. However, I knew that there was a difference between the two. Even though both countries have a similar topography and landscape, Korea is much more developed than China. The cause of such a vast difference was the people. Seeing the territory of Korea, I realized the important role of Christians.

The reward of the theology lecture: I have a new understanding of the symbolism of seventy years. Last month, I read Leviticus. I was touched by the fact that God wants us to live a pure life and learn to fear God. However, I didn't fully understand the symbolic meaning of the seventy years. From Jesus' point of view, the seventy years symbolizes freedom and independence. When I finally understood this principle, I was able to grasp the fact that Jesus Christ is at the heart of the Bible. Everything God has done is preparation for the birth and salvation of Jesus Christ. This has given me a deeper understanding of the gospel.

I was able to clearly understand the relationship among the woman, child, and the dragon in Revelation 12 in the context of the spiritual battle. I learned about Satan's position and ways in which he tests us. Satan was expelled from the heaven. He likes lies and deceptions. I finally became conscious that neither living in the wilderness nor living in the spiritual battlefield is a bad thing. This is because Jesus has already gained victory on the cross. When we rely on Jesus, we can win too. This is the greatest reward I gained from the trip to Korea.

I learned what serving others from the heart looks like. Without spiritual eyes, one can never see the needs of others. Without love, one cannot serve people from the heart. I asked God to give me the spiritual eyes and love to be able to see the needs of brothers and sisters in Christ, and to love them.

I also learned from Pastor Shin to have a strong faith that is not afraid of failure. We can build God's church anywhere the gospel can be shared. People like to disobey God; however, God looks for those who obey Him. God is patient and waits for people to change.

Pastor Shin's mentor Pastor Doh was a gentle and humble servant of God. He is a very famous leader of Korea missions, but he was so humble and gentle. He even drove us himself to our lodgings late at night. This is uncommon in China.

3. Application to individual life:

a. Deep consciousness of a pure life. I thought purity was simply about not committing cruel sins. However, now I understand that purity or holiness is a life marked by humility, obedience, and piety before God. I still lack in these areas.

b. The gospel is the beginning of blessing. Faith is the power to change one's life. One should put oneself down as well as one's attitude of self-reliance. One should learn how to completely obey God and depend on Him. How much God changes me depends on how much I rely on Him.

c. One cannot make up for failure in faith, but one *can* make up for failure in worldly matters.

It is by God's grace that I have received these lessons and insights. It will take a long time for me to understand and apply them in my life. I am grateful to God for His grace toward me and the teachings I have received through many people

8709419R0

Made in the USA
Charleston, SC
07 July 2011